Anticipate Every Goodbye

The award-winning account of the death of his mother by the French priest-novelist Jean Sulivan

Translated by Eamon Maher

VERITAS

Published 2000 by Veritas Publications
7/8 Lower Abbey Street
Dublin 1

ISBN 1 85390 540 2

British Library Cataloguing
in Publication Data.
A catalogue record for
this book is available
from the British Library.

Cover design by Bill Bolger
Printed in the Republic of Ireland by Betaprint Ltd, Dublin

Rien de plus pauvre qu'un enfant
Rien de plus pauvre que sa mère
Rien de plus pauvre qu'un soldat

– Paul Eluard

FOREWORD

I cannot ever forget the first time I heard of Jean Sulivan. It was on a warm August evening, during dinner at one of the little sidewalk restaurants lining the narrow streets near Place Monge in Paris. Shortly before that, I had by chance run into Eamon Maher outside the Irish College on Rue des Irlandais, a corner of Paris well trodden by succeeding generations of Irish scholars, poets, artists and student priests.

Like many before him, Eamon had been using the college as a Parisian base from which to conduct research for a doctorate on a French subject within the milieu of the French environment. While a busking tenor saxophonist played Piaf melodies to entertain us diners along the rue Mouffetard, Eamon began to enlighten me about the life and writings of Sulivan, the subject of his recent studies. The more he spoke of him, the more I wanted to know about this relatively little-known French author, philosopher, critic and priest. Regrettably, it was no longer possible to meet him in person – Sulivan died in 1980 – but at least, through his writings, it would be fascinating to encounter the ideas and opinions of a man whose critique of contemporary Western society, and the role of Church people within it, struck a resonance with my own observations, which I had never been able to articulate, even to myself.

We can be grateful to Eamon Maher for introducing this work of Jean Sulivan to English speakers. *Anticipate Every Goodbye* is a deceptive book. At first, it appears to be an exercise in nostalgia, a gentle reflection on the influence of a mother in a busy priest's life. However, it proceeds, almost imperceptibly, to become a powerfully challenging reflection on what can happen to a believer, priest or not, who becomes too removed from his or her background. Sulivan believes that he eventually came to understand his relationship with his Church through his relationship with his aging mother. In Sulivan's thinking, that is a much more complex observation than it appears to be at first sight. He became very wary of subtly masked prejudice and the self-satisfaction that can result from clever language.

Like many others, he was happy when his whole life was contained in a narrow thought system. He had answers to all the questions and was amazed that nobody would listen to him, so rigorous was his logic. With rapier-like use of words, Sulivan claims that Divine love was just a weapon in his hands, and describes himself as being the servant of a religion that was too focussed on itself, and he didn't even know it.

This book should be required reading for all lecturers, teachers and preachers, especially those who think they are good at it, and for whom the congratulatory 'You were brilliant' reaction is a recurring response. The author, obviously speaking from experience, points to the danger of making a career out of announcing the Gospel, and the feeling of helplessness when a sincere listener, touched by the sermon, asks afterwards, 'What do you think *I* should do?'

On a wider scale, this is a book that can throw light on many of the great questions that confront religion in contemporary society. In his reflections on the place of the Spirit and the essence of religious belief, the author bares his soul courageously and in doing so, defies the reader to do likewise, as he says, 'perhaps in the very secret hope that I will meet soul-mates who are scattered on other roads'.

In belonging to a Church that has thousands of years of organisational politics behind it and therefore has, in many ways, become over-confident in its certainties and decrees, Jean Sulivan writes, not to edify, not to cause scandal, nor simply to defend his ideas; he is merely describing what was and is an integral part of his consciousness. His thinking is that the obstacles upon which he stumbled are also those that prevent many 'abandoned' people of our time from advancing in inner knowledge.

To live out the paradoxes of the Gospel takes courage. Because he believed that he didn't have such courage, Sulivan admits that he bought into the whole religious culture thing. He found his niche and his escape route in culture, which saves a person while allowing him to stay on the surface of things. He could present dogma in a modem form, quote from the experts, hide behind Papal pronouncements, explore literature and the new world of cinema in order to find the correct symbols, the lessons learnt by others, but he was doing so only to preserve the illusion that he was truly expressing the core of his belief and living by it.

There is a searing honesty about this work. You read it in awe of Sulivan's ability to first of all identify the different strands of belief, to separate them from the sham and the pretentious, and to then communicate his findings to us in clear, almost blunt language. Time and time again, as I read it for the first time, I felt that Sulivan was articulating exactly what has been churning around in my own head for years – questions that have been the subject of many late-night discussions with believers of all shades and none.

His use of language too is fresh and colourful. Like his former compatriots of the pointillist school of neo-Impressionism, Seurat and Signac, Sulivan manages to build up a complete canvas of his stream of consciousness using tiny dots of key words that convey an overall lightness of touch and sparkling originality. It is a tribute to Eamon Maher's ability that none of Sulivan's vividness of language in the original French has been lost in translation.

Prophets make uneasy company. They prick our consciences, prod our certainties, oblivious to and often regardless of their consequent unpopularity. But we need them, if only to stimulate and force us to rethink our core values and beliefs. Jean Sulivan will be regarded by some as a rebel, a troublemaker, a dissident priest using his pen as a weapon of destruction. But, with this timely translation into English, Sulivan, like the prophet Amos coming into the Northern Kingdom bearing only a branch of sycamore, is enabled to make us once again question our certainties, and strip away the accretions that hide from us the face of God.

This foreword is just a thumbnail sketch of Jean Sulivan and his work, a mere appetiser. Now read on and enjoy the main course!

Dermod McCarthy
Editor
Religious Programmes – Television
RTÉ

I used never used to dream, or at least I was never conscious of my dreams. In a dream that recurs a lot recently, mother is ill, dying, dead. The harsh ringing of the phone awakens me. Dreams are designed to protect one's sleep: I am scarcely aware of the phone ringing to stir me from this particular reverie. I am irritated by this mechanism that operates within me and is outside my control. Every Sunday, when I go to visit my mother, the village tower still rises to meet my glance as I reach the top of the last hill. It's a high tower, heavy and square, with a bell-turret at every corner. Bushes grow as in the past in the gap between the tower and the roof. It was constructed at the end of the last century and, as was the case with many country churches that date from that time, they only knew how to imitate, pretend, give homage to God by impressing people through the trappings of power. As a child I had been impressed with our tower. It could be seen from anywhere in the vicinity like the bell-towers of Martinville. The villages around us had only very insignificant towers.

Now we come to the cemetery, the valley of Jehoshaphat as mother calls it, and the notice that the local authorities have attached to the wall:

> *A warm welcome to industrialists*
> *This area awaits your coming*
> *Attractive conditions available for anyone wishing to set up business*
> *here*

At mother's funeral, I will go to the front of the cortège, being the eldest in the family. I can already hear the grating of the wheels on the gravel, the sound of stupid optimism, the song of the solitary bird flying above the sea:

In paridisum
Deducant te angeli

Two hundred metres farther up, on the left, almost in the shadow of the high tower, beside the main road on which mad drivers chase after each other at breakneck speed, just after the boarding school, is our house. A slight pang of pain hits me at the mention of this.... One day the shutters will be closed. Everything's alright this time round. I can make out mother's shadow moving about through the curtains. 'You're a little late today,' she says, 'I'm frightened by those cars.' Or else, 'Ah, you're early.' We are always hesitant when we get to within two steps of one another. *Anticipate every goodbye, as if this goodbye were already behind you.* I kiss her on the forehead at the start of her hairline. We're not too demonstrative in our family. Those people who lift their arms in the air, throw themselves on each other, shake each other, exchange kisses and exclaim how well you look, you're getting younger every day, you're putting on weight, getting thin, we love you, we're always thinking about you – they scare me. The minute after they have indulged in this show of affection, they're empty, as dull as dishwater. I kiss my mother at the root of her hair. I will kiss her like this on her deathbed. She won't return my kiss, no more than she does now; that is the custom we have adopted. Everything takes place on the inside.

I don't hate Sundays because of this stop in the place where I was born. The telly is on. While moving around, mother listens to the Reverend Father from La Tour-Maubourg. Priests have the upper hand when it comes to people like my mother: they have taken on this sad and assured tone which was new fifteen years ago. She knows that I am about to flee to the garden, anticipates my irritation, turns off the telly. I should have been patient, endured the idea that mystery can be offered in the form of a spectacle, put up with the suave voice of the priest who talks for everyone and for no one. We go out together to inspect the garden, the state of the lawn, the trees, the flowers. The slugs are giving me an awful time of it, I'm going to cut down your peach-trees. If you had only listened to me, I told you that only the peach-trees from this area bear fruit, leave them for another year, mother. Look, all the cats in the country go through the hedge, am I going to feed the birds for the benefit of the cats? The petunias are running riot in the alleyways, the sunflowers are invading the vegetable plot, the rose shrubs are still finding it difficult with all the diseases to which they are susceptible. We walk in the loud noise of the bells of the high tower. Indiscreet bells, we have to shout to make ourselves heard. Scarcely has the last bell sounded for high-Mass than it starts up again to announce a baptism, then a death. Mother tells me that such and such a person has a grand-daughter – but you do know him well – another person has died. I don't know anyone in the area anymore. I pretend to know what she is talking about.

The time for the meal arrives.

'I smelt the roast, mother, you know. And the cabbage, the carrots, the leek, the turnips.'

'You will be happy, I have a galette today. I'll go and get the cider.'

'I forbid you to go down to the cellar!'

'You're giving me orders now, are you? Do you take me for an old woman?'

I have begun to be fearful of everything, the staircase that has been too well-waxed, the attic, the cellar, the iron wires that lurk in the alleys, the rocks. What if she broke her hip! My fears are magical, they make up for my absences. The bells have finally fallen silent. We eat in the kitchen, she with her back to the window that overlooks the garden, I opposite her. We ritually go through the food on the table. She talks about what the weather has been like, her fears. They no longer really concern her personally, but she likes to be a part of them. There will no longer be enough for the animals to eat, the weather is too dry, the land is too wet, the farmers will not be able to start sowing, the storm has ruined the corn; it's a disaster.

'It will recover, mother.'

'It's too late now.'

'The prices have gone down, they have gone up, but of course everyone has already sold.'

'You are always fretting; every year you predict a catastrophe. Still, no one goes under. You can see that.'

'That's the way I am made, she says. We were poor.'

She can see that I'm in a hurry. All the meals taken in communal refectories have taken their toll on me. I can't slow down my eating patterns. I'm not sure that the seasons, the crops, the village rumours interest me that much. I should have listened to you, mother. The afternoon drags on. I sweep from one room to the next, I start taking notes, I write at one end of the table, I am somewhere else.

'You're always scribbling, writing away. What can you be writing?'

'It's my profession.'

I'm bordering on anger. I should have tried to explain more often. But we speak a different language. Compared to my mother I am like a black man from Niger who, having been to Paris, goes home to his village, his hut, and doesn't know anymore how to sit on the ground, eat with his fingers. His car is at the door, he feels close to those around him, in solidarity with them, he could cry: the words no longer make any sense.

'Are you leaving already?'

'I have a book on the way: I must work on it.'

'How can you spend all your time writing?'

'It isn't that simple: I have to place myself in a silent setting, be alone and wait. I might do nothing, but I have to be on hand in case the inspiration comes. Do you understand?'

'It's difficult, she says. What a life you're making for yourself. You never meet anyone.'

See you next Sunday so, yes, next Sunday. I glimpse her outline in the French-window. By the time I have opened the door of the car and turned it around to set off for home, she has closed the door and she then raises the curtain with her right hand. With her left hand she waves goodbye, moving it gently from right to left, left to right. She only does this once, her face is lost in the window, I raise my right hand to signal goodbye. And now there is but one Sunday, one goodbye.

My mother is beautiful, I have only become aware of this fact in recent years. It's late in life to make such a realisation, very late. I had never really formed an image of her in my mind. It can be dangerous to form an image of what you love. For a great part of your life your

12

mother is like the air that you breathe, the rock on which you repose your tired body, the shade in which you take refuge under a tree. Besides, I wanted to think of myself as having no father, no mother, no country, to be from nowhere or from every place where I had friends. I was afraid lest the air disappear, that's all, lest the shadow become invaded with light. Then came the time when, in between my lengthy journeys, I left the city every Sunday morning to head back towards my birth. I didn't dare go abroad anymore, because of Sundays.

At seventy-five years of age she still had long, dark brown hair that she used to wear in a large bun. She hadn't a single white hair in her head. On one particular Sunday I was surprised to come across the picture of my mother as a young woman which had long since gone unnoticed in the attic. It was an enlargement in a gold frame that looked like it had been taken the day before and which had survived the upheavals of moving house, among so many other familiar objects, the clock, children's toys, dangerous mementoes associated with former emotional ties. Her face looked stern in it, a little proud, darkened by the heavy mass of hair that protruded above the forehead. She was wearing a long solemn-looking dress that opened at the top to reveal the white triangle of her blouse and finished in a stiff wimple around the neck. She was wearing a long gold neck-chain onto which a small watch was attached. If you added a parasol, or a lorgnette, something like that, she would have fitted perfectly the image of the grand lady of times gone by. Her look seemed as if it had never been visited by thoughts of either death or life. I rush downstairs impulsively, I brandish the portrait: this is you, Angela, I mouth off. She raises her eyes, her face stiffens, a tear forms at the edge of her left eye.

'I don't like photos,' she said. 'Take it away.'
This was the first sign.

For the last couple of years my mother had ceased being *natural*. I know why this was the case. She had become my friend, almost an accomplice. Before this time I had never gone back over my childhood and had never paid much attention to her stories. Now I questioned her regularly, while being careful not to open up any old wounds. I looked at her eyes, I listened to the sound of her voice. I was proud of her long dark hair, of how alert she appeared, of her *joie de vivre*. I could be writing a novel, a story, anything, and suddenly I would be shocked to observe that I was talking about her secretly.

That Sunday I helped her to rediscover the child she had once been. To go to school she had to walk four kilometres down a path that went under the railway line, at the Landauzie bridge. At midday she would eat with the elderly Tiercelin sisters. These two spinsters were relations, very holy people. From the threshold of her house mother could see the large bourgeois house they lived in, at the other side of the street, beyond a large garden opposite the high square tower. This branch of the family had become rich. Old man Tiercelin had been a farm bailiff. It was often said that he had earned his money dishonestly. Mother would still even say this in a hushed voice. He had taken the law into his hands too quickly, mother, he had been ahead of his time. Everything had ended up badly for the Tiercelin family.

The happiness of evil people ebbs away like a mountain stream.

Mother knew pages of *Athalie* off by heart. She had a biblical interpretation of things. Every Sunday evening her father would read a chapter from a holy book for his children gathered around him. She has one over me when it comes to the Old Testament, or when something comes up about Esther or Athalie. She would never have thought to question the rights of the landed gentry who, little by little, would see their power slip away from them. Besides, with a few rare exceptions, the local lords were the most solid supporters of religion. She couldn't see that they clung to this so as not to go under completely. In those times men killed each other less often in order to ensure an artificial type of existence for themselves, or in order to follow numerous ambitions that render life sordid and miserable. All they wanted was to survive. Poor people are not of necessity miserable. Miserable people still exist but poor people are as rare as a four-leaved clover. The insolence of luxury is displayed in front of their homes. All we have now are those who-have-not-yet-become-rich, those who are pressurised by advertising with its seductive imagery, tormented by a thousand desires, constantly humiliated by the morgue that is formed by those who have 'made it'. Alas! it is no longer a desire for justice that stokes up rebellion, but simple envy, to such an extent that all that happens is that you slip from one form of oppression into another. I believe that in mother's resignation there was this innate awareness, an instinctive knowledge that men's social position or their possessions were unimportant unless they were able to gear their existence towards its ultimate goal. She had told me so clearly one day.

'An idea came to me during the sermon, do you think it's right to follow a separate line of thought during a sermon? Anyway, I began to think that what happens in life is largely unimportant. Life is just a test to prepare us for . . .'

She was more perturbed by the new landed gentry emerging in the small towns who seemed to be amassing fortunes in a poor area, in an extremely limited sector.

'How can it be possible?' she would ask.

She wasn't passing judgement on them, merely expressing her fear.

'Mother, it's impossible to administer justice on your own. Take a doctor, for example. If he doesn't develop his client base, his business will fail. It would be necessary to change the system. But would the new one of necessity be any better?'

She shakes her head. I see that she doesn't believe me. In her view you can be honest in all possible circumstances.

'From the legal perspective, they are honest. They get rich legally. Real justice is something else altogether. Their Christianity consists of good deeds, the practice of their religion.'

'Well, in that case a new misfortune will engulf us,' she says.

In any case the misfortune had come to the Tiercelins. Cousin Tiercelin had been a 'good Christian', always on the side of the priests. He had become mayor. At that time the struggle between the Republicans and the Royalists was still intense. The Republicans weren't against religion *per se* but they were always suspicious of the priests whose sympathies invariably leaned in the same direction. The priests were poor. They did not seek out wealth for themselves but had a naive preference for the rich. Their greed was for the edification of the Church: they absolved themselves in this manner.

'I can still see us one day,' she says, 'at noon, coming out of catechism class, on the path of Prayer.'

On one side of the road you have the orphanage, the church, on the other side the public school. Nothing has changed.

'I can still see us throwing stones at one another on the path of Prayer. An altar boy's little bell rings and suddenly we see the choirmaster dressed in red rushing ahead of the priest in his surplice who is bringing the Blessed Sacrament to a dying parishioner. On both sides of the path everybody kneels down, makes the sign of the cross. Scarcely has our Lord passed by than we start fighting and shouting at each other again.'

A Republican had the nerve to stand in the election for Mayor. To make matters worse, he beat our cousin Tiercelin. What was his name? In any case, his triumph was short-lived. He died the following year, having repented of his sins. He received all the sacraments. Everybody had been trying to ensure the winning back of his reprobate soul. Madame Tiercelin had just given birth in the house located underneath the shadow of the church tower. When she heard the bells ringing out to announce the end of the funeral service, all her joy at seeing her enemy consigned to the earth made her get up out of bed to pull back the curtains. The effort killed her.

The story of another member of the Tiercelin family prolongs the conversation. I can see the scene through my mother's eyes. She must have been playing around the church. Was there no school? Perhaps school was over and she was going through the village on her way home to the farm. It was a warm summer's day. This particular member of the Tiercelin family, a lawyer, was working in his office. The window on the ground floor was open. A carriage pulled up outside, a man jumped out of it, rushed towards the window and gave the hapless lawyer three bullets in the head. The horse reared up on its hind legs and made to gallop off. The man leaped up and clung on to the head of the horse. He then jumped into the carriage and, from a standing position, gripping the reins tightly, he whipped the horse over and over again. It must have been one of Tiercelin's customers who felt he had been cheated out of an inheritance. 'An ill-gotten gain brings no profit', mother said. She was always mixing up Holy Scripture with proverbs. It is true, however, that there are proverbs in Scripture.

I have just followed the path that my mother took to go to school and I now know the garden from which she supposedly stole the prunes that she hid in one of the numerous ricks of hay on the farm. She would admit to this little misdemeanour in confession. It was on this same path that one evening she met Fr Massenal, the parish priest, a man with a great passion for hunting blackbirds, who was out with his dog and his walking stick. The pockets of mother's pinafore were full of prunes. She took fright, blushed guiltily. The parish priest was a short man with long white hair. He placed his hand on mother's head and said, 'Don't you know, Angela, that prunes which fall on the road belong to everyone. I can tell you this, dear, I'd love to still be at the age when I used to steal prunes.' Then suddenly he gestures to her to be quiet. He aims between the branches. The young girl can see up in the tree the red eyes of the blackbird who is hatching the eggs in her nest. She would like to cry out a warning to the poor bird. Stealing prunes off the road is no sin, killing birds in their nest is a good deed. He was an authoritarian sort, this little parish priest, or so it would seem. The stiff Roman collar would never leave his neck.

One day the Archbishop, wanting to engender some spiritual fervour among his flock after receiving letters of protest from some parishioners, announced publicly that he would hear confessions in the parish on the eve of the feast of the Assumption, which that year happened to fall on a Sunday. During his sermon, the Sunday prior to this, Fr Massenal announced that His Grace would be paying the parish the singular honour of coming to hear confessions. But, added the wily priest, as we were dealing with a person of the highest rank within the Church, he would only be hearing those with mortal sins on their conscience in the confession box on the left of the choir. He, for his part, would hear confessions on the right. As people assembled at the scheduled time it was noticeable that a long queue formed on the right. Nobody went to see the Archbishop.

The school path went underneath the railway tracks. The bridge at this point was called Landauzie bridge. Mother would wait under the bridge to hear the loud sound of the wheels as they went by.

Un jour je fus
A la Landauzie
Le train passit
Y m'écrasit. *

I noticed that my mother's songs come back to me more and more now. These simple songs were born of the earth itself. In those days poor people were not always glued to the television with it's ready-made refrains, which are for everyone and for no one. She used to sing *The Good Soldier Pitou*, every verse of which ended with the line:

Le devoir avant tout, le devoir avant tout. †

And then during Lent there were the religious songs: *Au sang qu'un Dieu va répandre . . . Ah chrétiens, mêlez du moins vos pleurs.* ‡ Her voice seemed to fill the farm, to be coming out of the walls. I approach her furtively, I lean against the door of the stable. I see her sitting on the stool, I hear the milk splashing into the light-coloured copper basin. The creamy milk flows freely, filling the basin. Mother's head is leaning forward, her forehead pressed against the side of the cow, as she sings:

Au sang qu'un Dieu va répandre.

Or sometimes it's a lament that I remember. The lament of Hélène Jégado, evil Hélène Jégado who nursed sick people in order to poison them, such was her fascination with dead people.

Qui pourrait chrétiens fidèles
Ecouter sans frémir
Un récit qui fait pâlir

---

* One day at the Landauzie bridge, / The train passed and ran me over.
† Duty first, duty first.
‡ To the blood that God is about to shed, / O ye Christians, / Join your tears at least.

Mille actions criminelles?
Pour des forfaits aussi grands
Est-il assez de tourments? *

She also sang about the wandering Jew:

Est-il rien sur la terre
Qui soit plus surprenant
Que la grande misère
Du pauvre juif errant?†

Or the canticle of Jehanne containing twenty-one verses all of which
end with the line: 'Tout passe'.

Sous le firmament
Tout n'est que changement
Tout passe.
Tout flétrit et s'efface
Comme la fleur des champs,
Tout passe.‡

Sometimes she would hum funny tunes that were composed at the
time in every village about local happenings:

Monsieur le Curé ne veut pas
Que M'sieur D'Villers soit maire.

---

* Who could listen, / you loyal Christians, / without fear and trembling / to a story that
renders insignificant / a thousand criminal deeds. / For such serious crimes, / is any
punishment too great?
† Is there anything on earth more shocking than the great sadness of the poor old
wandering Jew?
‡ On God's earth, / all things are in constant flux, / everything withers and fades away. / All
things fade and disappear, / like the flower in the fields, / everything withers and fades away.

Mais il ne défend pas
Que ce soit Monsieur Gillois. *

The poor are not much more important than old tools or other implements that no longer serve any real purpose. The story of their existence interests hardly anyone. But history doesn't forget them when it needs to highlight heroism, greatness or sacrifice. Whatever small amount they have to lose is snatched from them in this way. However, precisely because they are poor and vulnerable, they are more pure than rare and precious stones.

Mother's first real blow to her happiness was inflicted on a train, the Sunday before war (the First World War) was declared. A pilgrimage for peace had been organised at the shrine of Saint Anne of Auray. Her brother, a priest, was with her. Mother always loved pilgrimages, which never failed to uplift her, but in a very secret, sometimes cruel way. I believe that she knew almost instinctively that you didn't pray to change the world but to change yourself in the face of the world.

The train stopped at La Brohinière, a small railway station with little in it other than a few houses scattered around flat fields. My uncle got off the train and jumped back on excitedly clutching a newspaper. 'There's going to be a war!' he exclaimed.

My mother would later explain to me: 'Your uncle was as happy as a young schoolboy. He was trying hard to hide his joy but the effort was beyond him. "We'll go to Berlin", he declared.' Through the windows of the train the shape of the trees began to grow indistinct, as if covered by a mist. The voices that reached her were speaking a foreign language.

I can conjure up in my mind's eye my childlike uncle, full of the lion-hearted courage of youth. He was a prisoner of the dark war machine without even realising it. War is all about action,

---

* The parish priest does not wish Monsieur D'Villers to be mayor. But he is not opposed to the idea that it be Monsieur Gillois.

camaraderie. They were very lucky at that time to be able to marry Christianity and duty with the desire to lead and to be a hero, in an unquestioning manner. I'd say my uncle had a highly successful war. He signed up for a commando unit, escaped once or twice from the Germans, was showered with citations and medals galore, and finished up with the rank of captain. When the war was over he got terribly bored. Hunting, long walks in the mountains, these didn't satisfy his hunger for action. In between the First and the Second World Wars he went on military training exercises to keep himself fit for the next conflict. Even if he didn't much like the socialist in Péguy, he was still in awe of the writer who brought together so well the idea of the Gospel going hand in hand with the Fatherland, the notion that the Catholic Church and France were one and the same thing. One summer, during one of his many stints in the reserves, he came to our house dressed in full military uniform. He reminded me of a character from one of the many films made on the First World War. I asked him, 'What film are they showing?' He was hurt by my comment. Mother, who bought into the ideas of the time, was hurt also. It's not right to shove your beliefs down other people's throats. They can only be communicated through friendship. But sometimes you feel so alone and so you attempt to protect your new belief system by going on the attack. In any case my uncle got his second chance at war. It would be a brief experience for him this time round. He ended up a commander or colonel in the reserves, something like that. He died a sad man in his bed, saying to himself that all the values he had espoused in his life had disappeared. It wasn't his fault that he had been taught to revere those values.

But let's get back to the image of my small fragile mother, as white as a sheet, who had recently been wed, rolling through the countryside with my uncle saying to her, 'We'll go to Berlin!' At Questemberg, when the train had taken on as many pilgrims as it could fit, some people were saying the rosary, others singing hymns:

Sainte Anne, ô bonne mère,
Toi que nous implorons,

Entends notre prière,
*Et bénis tes Bretons.**

'I know you can't understand these things, son, and that you'll laugh at me when I say that I was no longer afraid. I sang along with the others.'

At the shrine of Saint Anne in Auray she climbed on her knees to the top of the high flight of steps that leads to the basilica. Several years later in Auray I would climb, by her side, another flight of steps at the top of which is situated the monument with the engraved names of hundreds of thousands of heroes and martyrs. But I was always bored by these pilgrimages and felt at the time that the dead of that war had nothing to do with me. Oh, when I think of my mother's poor knees! One day, before I die, God permitting, I will join in with all the other pilgrims and climb on my knees the steps that have been made smooth by the poor people who have climbed them. God, I would like to go towards you in a long procession of pilgrims. One day I would like to forget the fact that words have long been abused: I would like to resurrect the simple language of the primitive tribes and go forward towards You in prayer with the humble and the poor and forget about all the nonsense spouted to make people obey the Church's teaching.

After this episode you could say that mother didn't think any more about the war. When she got home, the next week passed uneventfully. It must have been around harvest time, the same time as when I write now, in this man's house where I have chosen to hide my pain from the outside world, looking out on grid-like fields that extend as far as the horizon. I can hear the sound of the combine harvesters getting clogged up and then starting up again – the straw is too moist this year.

Work was all that mattered, people had neither radios nor televisions then. The alarm bell went off one Saturday evening. It could have been a fire. On the farm of the newly married couple,

---

* O Saint Anne, Our Holy Mother, / we beseech thee, / hear our prayer, / and bless your beloved Bretons.

which was situated two kilometres from the village, there was little or no thought of war.

That Sunday morning my father was very late coming back from Mass. I see once more the distressed face of my mother as she recounts all this to me; she has her back to the window. It's a Sunday afternoon, our meal is over and she keeps on talking. 'I really didn't think you were interested in any of this . . . there was a time when you . . .'

I'm surprised myself by my interest. Why, in recent times, have I been so anxious to find out these things? I can see her eyes looking at me, the same look that she must have had fifty years ago, when I myself had not yet come into this world, as she waited behind the window panes, anxiously surveying the footpath for any sign of my father. Finally she sees him coming out from under the chestnut trees. He lifts the gate, pushes it forward, then brings it back carefully to its original position that has been carved out of the trunk of a tree. She goes out of the house, walks towards him. 'Death was already on his face', she told me. Mother doesn't so much recount as relive this episode. I now read death in her eyes, as she herself had seen it on that pathway. My throat is full of emotion as I write this, now that I know that I'll never see her face again. Because you are always at a remove from someone else. What difference would it have made had I gone over to her, wiped her tears? You never live in the present. The present only leaves us with an image of the past which we relive painfully. We are always a bit distant from what we cherish, we move away at the critical moment. Writing is like loving twice over, suffering the same grief a second time. Years later I took the same path to go to school, I came back among the corn and the oats. The path has disappeared now. The bulldozers have removed the chestnut trees.

'We're always afraid, mother, and when events confirm our worst suspicions we say: I knew it. If nothing happens, we forget about it'.

'You are able to come up with an explanation for everything,' she said.

The only reason I explain things or become ironic about them is to escape this deeper world into which she has gone in the hope of dragging me with her. While she goes on with her story, I imagine this unknown father, and see through his eyes the face of his young wife coming towards him. They stop a couple of feet from one another. He is carrying the twelve pound loaf of bread that was popular at the time. The bread escapes from his hands, falls on the ground, stays in the space between them, while they look at each other already from a great distance.

Anticipate every goodbye as if this goodbye were already behind you.

Years later, on the same overgrown path, I saw the agony of Dinan, our colt. Mother was crying. Losing a horse spelt ruin at the time. His long legs were trembling, a long shudder could be seen going down his red-coloured coat. You could see the sky and the chestnut trees reflected in his stony gaze. The eyes of dying animals are terrible to behold. One would almost believe that they are speaking to you. All that is needed is a good translator. I can see mother's hand closing the colt's eyelids. She must have still been alone at that stage. She hadn't yet remarried. There were just the two of us and a few people hired to help out on the farm. Dinan's death was the fault of one of them called Zizi. He had made the poor thing gallop after giving him his feed of corn and hay. 'It wasn't your fault', mother comforted him 'Nobody taught you how to . . . '
'You really loved Dinan, do you remember?' she says to me. 'Afterwards you went to hide in the attic. You gave me such a fright that I forgot all about the colt.'

My father left on Tuesday morning in search of glory. He wanted to go to the station on his own, across the fields, with his army-issued pack slung over his shoulder. I am proud of the fact that this stranger didn't talk about going to Berlin and had no notion of becoming a hero. I suspect that as he was heading to the station across the paths he was saying goodbye to the land with the soles of his shoes. I also have an image of him passing his hand lightly over the trunk of a tree with, perhaps, the same look of not knowing what would become of him as I saw in the eyes of the dying animal. I don't think I've ever seen the news reels of the First World War without closing my eyes in shame. It's almost as though the soldiers could see themselves, as if I were among them, these men who were rudely torn from their humble existence, these puppets tossed about in the communication trenches, blessed by their priests, robotic soldiers bolstered up by alcohol as much as by the monstrous propaganda campaigns which confused everything: money, fatherland, religion, God. It is always the living who recall the wars. At times you'd like to have the perspective of those who died. Obviously they have become too serious or too light-headed to have a point of view.

The loyal soldier wrote home every day. On the mornings when there was no letter, the postman did a detour to avoid being seen empty-handed. Mother would raise the curtain on the window, go outside and down the path a little bit. Then she'd come back in and raise the curtain once more to wait as she had waited that first Sunday morning after war had been declared.

'Ah, now I remember the postman's name. He was called Chauvin. It was so long ago . . .'

Old Chauvin used to hide behind a tree until mother had gone back into the house and then he'd cross over quickly, like a thief in the night. The only problem was that there was a dog on the adjoining farm who would bark at the postman. Mother guessed early on what was happening but she would never let on, not for anything in this world.

Should a letter arrive on the evening train, this kind man, although he had already covered the fifteen kilometres of his round on foot, would head back up to our farm so that mother could sleep with an easy mind. He liked a drop of alcohol. The combination of alcohol and tiredness made him into a prophet. He'd say: 'I have to carry too many things in my bag, Angela, or sometimes not enough. Some day they'll skin me alive. All these telegrams arriving, the fear, the tears and the blood that they bring. The whole thing will end in a terrible mess, mark my words!' I couldn't have failed to meet this postman in later years because he lived for a long time after that. I ought to have paid more attention to him, kissed his feet for having been so kind to mother. But when, as an adolescent, mother would try to talk to me about these things I wouldn't let her get past the first sentence. My heart was too full of knots.

The letters all said that my father, the soldier, was ready to die, as if he wanted his wife to gradually get used to the idea of his being dead

25

and that she would at least have the slight comfort of knowing that he had died in peace. I find that lately I have a desire to read the letters. But it's too late. Long since discouraged by my stubborn indifference, my mother ended up burning them.

Two months went by without any letter from her beloved. All these mornings she would go out and back into the house, raise the curtain, hear the dog barking at the postman as he did his rounds of the nearby farms. The rumour went out that there had been hundreds of thousands of soldiers killed in this or that place. On a certain Sunday morning one of the hired hands on the farm came back from Mass with the news: 'People are saying that the boss will not be coming back.' After High Mass mother headed into the grocery store. There a woman said to her in an abrupt manner, 'So it's true then that your man is already dead?' A wisteria plant surrounded the shop-window. I see in my mind's eye the jars of multi-coloured marbles and lollypops, the tuppenny sticks of liquorice in the shop-window, the little bell that rang for quite a long time to announce the arrival of each new customer. Mother went pale at the shock and collapsed beside the counter. The grocer, Reynaud, was an elderly man and his wife was a mousey sort of woman who wore glasses. They were both friendly with my mother. They carried her quickly into the back of the shop and gave her something strong to drink. Then the old man went out to hitch the horse up to the cart to bring my mother back to our farm, which was called Fontaines noires.

'Do you know something, in those days people were tougher than they are today,' she'd say. 'It's funny how people today have less religion and still they seem to me to be more vulnerable somehow. Maybe it's because they're more taken up with the radio and television and have nothing to talk about. What's your opinion on that, Mr Know-it-all?'

One night mother had seen her husband covered in blood as a huge hand was pinning a medal to his tunic. He got up and flung the medal in the mud, then dragged himself along the ground to try to find it again. But she had another vision that same night.

'It's not logical,' she said. 'You will not believe me.'

And still, when she checked the dates she thought that the night she dreamed about his death was the same as the date that he was killed and would subsequently receive his medal. The crows had been making a racket all day in the high poplars in front of the house. She had tried in vain to chase them away with stones. And this vision, which she only allowed herself to talk about guiltily and in a very low voice, had helped her more than anything, in her estimation, to find peace. For a long time afterwards, all she had to do was close her eyes and she could see a blinding light in the midst of interspersed rainbows and my father coming towards her joyfully saying, 'Don't be afraid anymore, the war is over, there is no more death.'

'I can tell you now, whether or not it was an illusion on my part, this vision made me very happy, so much so that I felt like singing.'

These last few years I have begun to wonder about the exact nature of my mother's relationship with me. I think she was a bit aloof, very unwilling to show her true feelings. It's as if she always remained at a certain distance from me. Is it possible to understand that? After all, some people are afraid to touch those they love and choose to think of them as absent before they have died. These same people talk to the dead as if they were alive. She had a strange look about her, my mother, one that plumbed the depths of your soul. You couldn't get her to stop for a moment to get a better look at her. She was like an ant, always on the go, always carrying things that were too heavy for her, tidying things away, dusting, waiting in fearful anticipation, determined to go back over familiar ground, to use the same gestures she had always used. Up until the last couple of years it was impossible to get her to stop.

There are times when it takes a whole life for the heart to turn to stone, for it to lose its protective shell and replace hope with a sad type of wisdom. You can see it in the faces of the people who have undergone this process; they assume a vacant look, like statues. But there are times when this process occurs as quickly as receiving a knife wound in the guts. Afterwards you walk in the middle of a deserted forest; you force yourself to say the conventional things but it is clear that you are somewhere else. The mutation can be permanent, or else the heart, which has benefited from a long sleep, can start wanting human contact again. The distance remains, however, as a result of some kind of protective defence mechanism against suffering. For a long time I had seen death in my mother's eyes and it is possible that I was fleeing from this sight. What is most strange is the fact that for several years my mother had appeared to be getting younger-looking. She was very keen to talk and laugh; she did less tidying.

'How can one suffer as much as I have done and still go on living?' she asked me one Sunday afternoon. 'How can I have suffered and yet be so happy in myself? Is it by chance? Misfortune has passed us by.'

Did I really hear the bells ringing to announce the armistice? Mother didn't think so. In the years after Armistice Day it is possible that they rang out to celebrate the anniversary. Whatever the reality was, I can still vividly remember the bells being rung loudly. The workers jump about excitedly in the yard, shout, throw their hats in the air. I can't believe that I would remember such joy if it were merely to mark an anniversary. Mother appears on the porch, very pale: everything is frozen in time for a second. She takes down the bronze basin and heads towards the stable. I follow her from a distance and stand guard at the door. I cannot hear the familiar sound of the milk splashing into the basin. I go closer. Mother is sitting on her stool with the basin on her knee. She has leaned her forehead against the side of the cow; the animal turns around to see what's happening. Suddenly mother looks up at me and her eyes are full of tears.

It was unthinkable to me at one stage to imagine the fact that it was with my mother that I first saw the sea. We had taken the train to Saint-Brieuc where our landlord lived. He was a doctor, he ran a small nursing home. He had summoned us to talk about the renegotiation of our lease. The picture of my frail mother comes back to me and I see her in this opulent and well-furnished office, at the edge of a leather armchair, her face displaying her anxiety, dressed in black as was her custom (to acknowledge past griefs and to anticipate all the catastrophes that awaited her). She pays what is due on the quarterly rent; she opens her handbag, takes out a large brown wallet, unfolds the notes, hands them to the landlord. The elderly gentleman extends his wizened hand to accept the money and then throws it in a careless manner into his roll-top desk. He was a tall, stiff-looking gentleman who had a white goatee which came down to a point below his chin. He played nervously with an old letter-opener and explained that he was going to have to double the rent.

'But please, sir, we won't be able to manage that.'

'My dear Angela, I know what problems you have but I also have a few of my own.'

Indeed he did have some problems: he had to buy a factory for one of his sons who was turning out badly. Everyone was going to have to pay for this rehabilitation. It was obvious that his tenant farmers would have to . . . There were no real laws protecting the poor at this time. My mother began to weep. I know that I was ashamed of her for a short moment. You only really feel guilty and ashamed if you are poor.

We were shown through the dining room, which was full of crystal, silverware of all sorts, tablecloths on all the tables. Grace was said in a solemn manner and there was a servant in attendance, dressed in his dark evening suit. Our landlord was a good sort, really, fair-minded and honest, that much was obvious. We went through to the sitting room; it was as beautiful as a church that awaits the congregation for Easter Sunday Mass. I got bored quickly, I kept pulling mother's sleeve. At last the landlord escorted us to the front door that led onto the street. I could tell that she didn't dare ask the question, that she was frightened, but I kept pulling at her dress. She took the bold decision eventually:

'What way should we set about going to the sea, sir? My son wants to see it.'

This probably moved the doctor. He called for a servant.

'Get the horse and carriage ready,' he said. 'I am giving you the afternoon off to bring our friends here to the seaside.'

And so off we set, mother and I in the back. We could see the driver through the glass partition with his high hat. Weren't rich people great all the same! The beach we went to was called Les Roseliers if I'm not mistaken. I didn't dare go too close to the sea.

When I am beside the sea or in the mountains I never seem to be too unhappy. It's as if I find in these places the cure for my problems in peace. The waves coming forward and receding, or the steep peaks that suddenly appear have a hidden meaning that it takes time to decipher. The sea invites you to seek out knowledge, the mountains tell you to leave everything behind you. There are times when it is right to go to the mountains; like when you need the will to break down barriers in order to see the light again. There are times also when you should visit the sea; when you need to contemplate on eternity, a process that can lead to peaceful serenity. The sea and the mountains use a language without words, that travels straight to the marrow of our being.

At the seaside mother was a frail, fragile-looking figure. She didn't want to get out of the carriage: there were too many well-to-do people there for her liking. I walked along the water, a few metres away from it. I didn't have the courage to go any closer, to bend over it. I thought everyone was looking at me so I pretended to be brave, proud, cock-sure of myself. Or maybe I didn't approach the sea out of a certain shyness, which I felt because my heart was moved by what I saw and I promised that one day I would come back and visit the sea again when there would be no one else around and then I could look at it to my heart's content, commune with its tumult. I walked as far as the end of the beach and, hidden behind a rock, I took up some water and put it on my hands and face: it was a type of baptism. The seashells and the algae allowed me to share in their dizzy happiness. The sharp cries of the seagulls pierced my heart. Since that time I have walked on beaches in the south of Italy, in Africa, in the Lebanon, even along the Indian ocean. I would only know later that what I experienced that first time was the marvels you can find in yourself, the throbbing of the blood running through your veins. I believe that each time I see the sea I experience the dizziness of that child dressed in his sailor suit whom his mother awaits in her black mourning outfit, a fragile silhouette etched in the sky above the beach. Had she already remarried at this stage? No, we wouldn't have come on our own to see the sea had that been the case. She might have been crying because of the increase demanded on the rent? Perhaps it was at this moment, in order not to leave the farm, that she decided to remarry?

She had the impression that I didn't enjoy my time at the seaside. 'You'd want to be a genius to know what pleases that young lad', she'd say. The first time I saw Venice I stayed there just an hour. If I'm captivated by a book I sometimes read twenty pages and leave it to one side for good and all. Beauty can hurt you, you have to deal with it in a cautious manner. You feel like dissolving into nothingness. I think that I could explain myself to her better now. At that time I didn't have the words.

I don't think I ever truly appreciated the awful time my mother was having. I was all caught up with myself, busy trying to realise a thousand desires immediately. Life can be kind to the child by protecting him with this shell of self-absorption. And yet the sight of mother's tears touched me deeply and it was possibly these same tears that would cause me to take instinctively, sometimes hypocritically, the part of the poor and the victims of this world.

There are certain images of my early childhood that don't arouse any emotion in me. When we're not aware of how things impact on us, when they lie dormant in us for years, they probably mark us all the more deeply. But it takes a long time for us to identify the feelings that make us behave in a certain way and to be cured of our many feelings of resentment. In any case it has certainly taken me a long time to acknowledge that modern civilisation has succeeded in achieving the paradox of changing the poor into the rich, to such an extent that the saying 'woe to the rich', which is not so much a curse as a true statement – 'the rich are unhappy' – extends to the poor who are frustrated in their ambition to acquire all the trappings of wealth. One day we get an insight which makes everything clearer and we begin to ask the real questions. How is it that the rich appear to be the best supporters of the Church? To me the most incredible, outlandish thing of all is how so many rich people can come on Sundays to receive Communion, to adore the One who was born in a stable, who was persecuted by the High Priests of the true religion, nailed to a cross like a common slave. How can they worship the One who said: 'The first shall be last. Prostitutes will enter the kingdom of Heaven before you'? The Christ who treated everyone equally, who was merciful, who was only ever brutal with one race of people, rich hypocrites. He chased the merchants from the temple and he never put any store by material possessions, or family background, or race. I suppose the miracle in all this is that among the rich and the poor who came to

31

wipe the slate clean, to worship in a safe way a historical figure, to clear their consciences of any thought of ill-doing, beyond the bleating of those who thought they were taking part in an opera, there were still a few who were capable of listening to the eternal Word, which is still announced today and which overcomes pride and social prestige and holds up as virtues humility and poverty of the spirit.

In order to achieve true happiness you need to follow the straight path that steers clear of the temptations of that world that encourages us to acquire and covet material goods. I have often experienced at first hand the unhappiness of the rich, an unhappiness that at first appeared to me to be a pious play on a deep irony. How can people divest themselves of their wealth? This is the question that it is necessary to put to a modern world which is preoccupied with one question and one question only: how can I get rich? My mother unknowingly taught me how to deal with this problem. This is why I have the courage to write about her. She's not just my mother but is the mother of all of you, the mother of times gone by.

In fact I discovered not just the sea but also the mountains with her. We did many things together. But I was absent from her, unbearable, as she often explained to me. About the pilgrimage she brought me on I can only remember the train from which you caught glimpses of beaches, a large river, acres and acres of pine trees. The smell of sausages and red wine filled the carriages. The priests are most relaxed, in an innocent sort of way, when they are in the company of women. They loosen their collars, become convivial even to the point of assuming a swagger. There's no end to the number of rosaries said and hymns sung.

> *Nous venons encore*
> *Du pays d'Arvor.* *

What was her reason for going to Lourdes? Because of a vow she had made when father headed off to war? As I have already said, she

---

* Here we come once more / From the land of Arvor.

knew that every prayer is always answered and that it is possible for faith to refer to our suffering as grace and mercy because suffering forces us to seek comfort from a higher source. I never saw my mother so happy as after the long, exhausting pilgrimages she went on all her life. Prayer was a tonic for her.

At the grotto I splashed water over my face. I even drank some of it. I wanted to become a saint because I had heard in a sermon that is was lovely, great to be a saint. It was like asking for glory and wealth. It is probable that I just wanted to be different. Sanctity was something that stole up on you by surprise. I drank too much water and it made me sick. After that I lost interest in the grotto in front of which mother never stopped praying, her face lit up by the joy of it all. I was untouched by the sight of the sick people lying on the stretchers or sitting in their wheelchairs. It is possible that they filled me with horror.

Many years later, on the only occasion I would come back to Lourdes, I felt the same need to flee. 'Those among you who are suffering are the blessed ones,' was the pronouncement made by the healthy-looking preachers. But among those who were suffering, even if there were a few saints in their number, there must have been some who were saying to themselves that they would much rather live a normal life, see, walk, than to continue with their suffering. They were brought around in their wheelchairs, exposed to the inquisitive looks of healthy people for hours on end while they waited under the hot sun for the procession to begin. The 'slings', as these stretcher-bearers were called, also got their reward; they were able to say the rosary while they pushed the wheelchairs or carried the stretchers. The sick person was obliged to reply to the prayers at the risk of receiving a reprimand. Those who were ill would have preferred to chat and make friends. This was out of the question. The crippled said countless rosaries. It would have been considered less than acceptable for one expression of human friendship to pass their lips.

But the time I went to Lourdes as a child with my mother all I felt were boredom and fatigue. We had an elderly cousin who was an invalid and who went every year on the train that was laid on for sick people: she loved going on trips. Any time we went to see her in hospital she'd moan, 'Cattle is all we are, Angela, nothing but cattle. I have the faith, that much I can promise you, but my stomach is sick from praying.' Mother was shocked at this outburst. So was I.

Nonetheless I am sure that I felt something approaching disdain for the men I saw praying for the sick people in front of the grotto, with their hands raised in a position that would make you think of the crucifixion, and with the rosary beads hanging from their right hand. And if I were to try and recapture the various and confused feelings I was having at the time it would probably go something like this: Didn't God make us all mortal? Why then try to change this? Why drag yourself along the ground, why make such extravagant gestures when it is surely possible to talk simply to God like you would talk to your mother? Who was God anyway? And if He was in the business of making exceptions why did he not make the exception the rule? What possible reason would I have to deny the possibility that God intervenes in the business of what He has created? The idea of the impossible making a sudden appearance appealed to me very much. I like to see logic being turned on its head. I have never seen anything, that's all. I suppose I have never really wanted to see such a thing. I would probably be disappointed in God if he started being spectacular in order to impress me. Miracles are everywhere, in the stunning beauty of life, in human gestures that say more than they are saying, in love that seeks to be eternal. I wouldn't like to feel hemmed in. However, I must confess that there was one time when I really wanted a miracle. Because life seeks to damp down our pride and to show us one day, even at a point in our lives when we have acquired a more accurate picture of the human condition, to show us sooner or later that we, like everyone else, have a soft spot in our heart. At that moment we shout and are surprised to hear ourselves begging for a miracle.

Every afternoon there was a huge procession of the Blessed Sacrament around the outside of the basilica. On seeing this I was filled with sadness and remorse. I should really be accusing myself for being lukewarm, for having bad thoughts. And what else, I ask myself? After all these years if now I have to be present at similar manifestations, especially if they happen to take place in the public arena, I have the same reaction, only now the guilt is gone. I pray to the Son of Man, to the Son of God, of that you can be certain. But more than any feeling of sadness I can feel rising within me an uncontrollable amazement, maybe even anger, at the thought that people can parade, show off in this ostentatious way the Son of Man whose presence, for reasons of divine humility, was concealed under the outward appearance of bread. It is my opinion that Jesus did not initiate the Eucharist for it to be displayed in triumphalist processions, but rather for it to be eaten like we eat the bread of the earth, not under the watchful eye of spectators, but with a few friends around a table. Nothing is really seen except when it is enveloped in mystery from within. The spectacle, the copes worn by the priests, the gold rim on the vestments, the incense holders, hide the real meaning of religious events more than they make them accessible. For a long time I felt very guilty at my relief when the great and spectacular religious services were over. I don't say these things in an attempt to excuse the ideas I have been expressing. I am merely describing what I felt. I don't always approve of my own opinions. I have made the pledge to myself that I will be truthful. It is not necessary 'to be blessed with religious beliefs' in order to be a good Christian or priest, this is something that a lot of lost souls of this era should know. But I had to undergo a period of suffering and pain before I came to the simple realisation myself that Christianity is not first and foremost a religion.

The mountains were what attracted me most to these pilgrimages to Lourdes. But the pilgrims who gave the impression of 'being out for the day' made my mother very indignant. It is true that for many the pilgrimage was only a pretext. One day I moved away from the grotto and started what I believed to be an ascent. The peak was right beside me, so I figured I would have completed my climbing expedition within two hours. When I returned to the hotel, red with embarrassment, having been picked up by tourists who had looked after me on the descent, it had been dark for a long time and everyone was asleep. Mother was nervously patrolling the front of the hotel: I saw the strain on her face, her look, the same look she probably wore on the path that first Sunday at the beginning of the War when she saw death in my father's eyes.

It was a very disappointing climb but I will never forget the mountains. And there is something else that I would never forget. This was the only place I had ever prayed from the depths of my heart, and in my own unique way, the universal prayer.

Childhood is so full of new experiences. I know that I would have difficulty giving more than a very brief sketch of my own. The adult always tries to invent what is beyond mere words. And if life doesn't allow us to hold onto or to relive one day something of the fullness or of the emptiness of childhood, this primitive sentiment of belonging somehow, the happiness at existing that is hidden at the heart of every living creature, then it is merely pretentious and sterile. In my opinion, the most deadly sin of all is a sad and providential sort of wisdom. Because life knows better than we where it is taking us. That is why our modern philosophers, who can't see from having their heads in the sand, who would like to have us believe that the ultimate wisdom can be found in rational reasoning and that faith can be found in the absence of faith, seem to me to lack above all else the spirit of childhood because they have cut themselves off from the life that carries within it unabashed hope.

There is nothing for the memory in all this. Days last for centuries. Vivid experiences come back to me in a very immediate way from my childhood: how we looked after the trees, our fondness for the animals, the freshness of the mornings, the fatigue that set in on warm afternoons, the hopeful expectation of where a road might lead to, the constant presence of my mother. I never go back in time in order to regret things, or to savour them. Fear is foreign to me when I undertake these steps backward in time. And if perchance I am ill, the process of memory is no longer within my control: the fever, the people looking after me are all part of the game of life. Death doesn't enter into it. Nor do thoughts or words attempt to break the day-to-day continuum, to brush you aside for good and all. And if your heart is made to suffer you are largely unaware of it: the images of what has happened to you lie dormant in some obscure part of your being. Everything is reduced to one summer, one bright, warm summer, just as now there is but one Sunday in spite of all these comings and goings over the past ten years when I tried, in a frightened way, sometimes annoyed with myself and with my mother, to rediscover the memories of my past.

My childhood reminds me of a dark room. I can see the flame of a holy candle flickering there. A storm is raging. Was my poor mother frightened? She did exactly as she had seen her mother do in similar circumstances. The candles during a storm are more knowledgeable than we: they tell us that man has created neither heaven nor earth. Mother's small outline comes and goes in the flickering of the flame.

I have ears that stick out; there's no cure for it. I'm your typical peasant. I knew from the way the hair stood up on the coats of the cows and the goats that it was going to rain. I was up at four o' clock in the morning. From Fontaines noires you had to go across the village to reach what was known as the *Grande Prairie de Séléhem* (Great Meadow of Selehem). You had to travel five kilometres to get there, along the bank of the meandering Garin river, which was a well-known spot for tench and roach. I was keen to be the first to wake up the village with the crack of my whip. I wanted them to say: 'Hey, there's young Sulivan going by already at this early hour.'

I had trained our animals to walk in a straight line, in twos, for no real reason other than to show off. I had different names for each of the animals: Gare, Décidée, Fleurie, Charmante, Luciole. Ah, when I think of all these long hours, mornings that would never end! I could doze off as I pleased, or read, or follow the traces left by skunks, otters and weasels.

Mother was upset when we had to send the animals away for slaughter. I can see the scene vividly – mother bent over with her left arm stretched forward, the forearm bent backwards to hold up her lustrous hair, while the right hand brought the comb through the hair.

'Can I comb it for a while?' I asked.

'Yes, you can, I don't feel anything. You could hang me up by the hair like Absolom and I wouldn't feel a bit of pain.'

You could hear the animals getting restless and making noise outside. They were probably unwilling to get into the trailers. I rushed to the window.

'Do you know where they're going?' she asked me.

To me it didn't matter. All I wanted was to see the struggle between the men and the animals. She, on the other hand, felt that they belonged to us. We all shared the one existence. The Indians are acutely aware of this truth and the poor experience it in whatever part of the world they happen to live.

It is difficult for me to imagine how I was once ashamed of being a peasant. I think that I may have been in some way protecting my mother. I was afraid lest people judge her on external appearances. In front of the *villotins,* as we called city folk, she would become dreadfully subservient. For her to shine, to tell stories, she needed to be among her own.

People have a particular way of looking at you. They say 'peasant' without realising that the word can have the same resonances as 'nigger'. People from the country are considered dense, from all the manual work they have to do in the fields. They are seen as tightfisted beings who love to lie in their own dirt. 'I'll tell you what; give them a bath and they'll raise rabbits in it! They prefer their animals to their wives, or their children!' The *villotins* don't necessarily say these things, but that is the way they think and it is expressed in their mannerly condescension.

Whether or not by choice, for a while with much delight and out of stupid vanity, I became a part of the the world of the pace-setters. It didn't take me long to feel like an outsider. They had their villas by the sea or in the mountains, their boats. They changed their cars every six months, moaned about the taxes they had to pay. I saw them through my mother's eyes, I can always recognise those who have drifted too far from their roots, those who spent their childhood among the poor and who remembered the trees around their houses, the animals they kept. They never quite get over their discomfort; they look sad. They have never fully reconciled themselves to thinking about their own interests solely; they aren't ready to lock themselves away in their little fortress. Some of them are even kind enough to give me the key to their dwellings. I am a sort of alibi for them, something they use to soothe their conscience. How would I even attempt to pass judgement on them? I contribute to their posturing. I am just a signpost which they come across along the road: I show them what way they should go but I don't follow the same path myself. The reason I write is to console myself over all these missed opportunities.

Three kilometres from the village, on the small road to Léléac, on the left, in an opening of the forest of Herminière, can be seen rising up in the distance the château called the 'Grand Manoir'. An avenue leads straight up, in the shade of twenty-year-old oak trees, to the side-gate. Like all the châteaux in the world, this one boasts a tower at each corner full of tiny slits, with the usual battlements at the top. Along the avenue can be seen a few piles of green-looking cannon balls, reminders of former conflicts that set young people dreaming about the past.

Three hundred metres further on you come across the dirt path leading up to the farm attached to the 'Grand Manoir': a muddy path broken by huge holes that would comfortably house a young calf. This is the path that we would follow, squashed into the cart with its huge wheels which made large imprints in the mud as we drove along, when we visited our aunts and uncles. From our farm, Fontaines noires, we would head there for family get-togethers, for meals that would take place at Christmas and Easter, for christenings and funerals. The courtyard of the castle, like the avenue, was covered in very fine sand. But the farmyard in winter was full of dry leaves, gorse bushes and genistas that would sometimes come up to your knees. The outhouses leaned against the castle walls. The farmhouse, as was the case with the sheds and the stables, had a thatched roof. You had a great contrast here between the poverty and misery of the farm buildings on the one hand and the splendour and grandeur of the thick walls of the castle on the other. On one side you had neatness, order and privacy, on the other noisy children with dirty noses. The division was stark between the farm labourers and the lords who were either comfortably relaxing in the castle or away on one of their many trips.

Around five in the evening, however, when it was time to milk the cows, the huge wooden door, surrounded by iron fittings that had been made not far from the castle, was opened, and you could see through the huge wall that separated the two courtyards. The contrast was also striking between the farmyard, with its numerous gorse shrubs growing wild and its rotting leaves, and the castle yard with its fine sand designed for delicate footwear and elegant dresses, the pond with the water-lillies and goldfish. Madame Désesseule's maid, who was called Maria, would come into the room with a jug of milk for us, and an old-fashioned basket full of food. She was a fine girl with a ruddy complexion who seemed to be born for cleaning out stables and energetically driving out the horses while she was performing this task. She was a farmer's daughter who gave the impression of being uncomfortable working in such splendid surroundings, without being required to even get her hands dirty. Among us simple folk she'd be back in her element, telling us endless stories about the goings-on in the castle. The previous evening there had been a reception that had attracted people from Rennes, maybe even from Paris, she wasn't sure. All the silverware had been placed on the tables and a bus had been laid on to transport the food from the nearby restaurant, *Au Faisan Doré*. The mistress had banished her daughter from the house because of some major argument over money. Very well-to-do gentlemen had told what could only be described as disgusting stories. At two o'clock in the morning the bus had transported all the staff and the materials back to the restaurant.

'I'll pay whatever it costs,' her mistress had said, 'as long as it's done quickly. At ten o' clock the following morning I don't want to see any signs of this reception.'

Marie would be kept busy for days on end cleaning up the mess left by those people. What's more, she was very frightened at night of the ghosts.

But often when Maria was gleefully recounting these stories, the gate would open again and her mistress would be heard to say:

'Maria, what are you doing in there? Hurry up!'

'I'm coming Madame, I'm coming,' Maria would shout from the stable door. And then under her breath. 'Oh, she'll give me a roasting for this, the old cow.'

And she'd run off in the direction of the castle. A moment later the key could be heard turning in the lock.

I was shocked by Maria. Through my childlike eyes, the Grand Manoir, on the castle side, was like a vision of paradise. Sophisticated, well-mannered and kindly people lived there. It was full of mystery with the music and the lights that you'd notice when there was a party on; the nimble-looking girls who were the stuff that dreams are made of. It all seemed part of a world that no longer existed. Underneath the high coachhouse you could see the small two-wheeled and Berlin coaches, the more elegant carriages that had a glass panel separating the driver from the passengers, coats of arms displayed on all of them, large silver door-handles. They were like things that should have been on display in a museum, witnesses of bygone splendours.

I found out later that Madame Désesseule threw her daughter out of the house because, or so the rumours went, she married an actor from the Opéra Comique, a former butcher with a most pleasing voice. Her son, Adhémar, must have been a student around this time. He was living it up in college and was rarely seen by us. During the Christmas holidays he went skiing and in summer he'd head off to Switzerland or on a cruise. He used to come for whirlwind visits on a powerful German motorbike with a young girl – never the same one – on the passenger seat with her hair streaming in the wind. He had all the arrogance of youth; he was like a God to me. In his eyes people like us didn't exist. I had no idea at that stage that one day we would become friends.

Years went by. Adhémar fell on hard times and had to sell the château to the local authorities. At present, kids on welfare placements live there and are ruining the place. The fine sand is no longer there, nor the goldfish. The ordinary people are taking back what was rightfully theirs in the first place, as some people would say. They grow potatoes in the lawns. The old oak trees on the avenue leading up to the castle have been cut down. The pond is being steadily taken over by the reeds. This is the same castle that we all dreamed about, a place full of marvels.

The mistress of the castle was absent on a regular basis. She was either in Rennes, in the winter, in her hotel that was located on the boulevard d'Acigné, or in Nice. In the summer she was to be found in Saint-Aulaire. During her absences we could pretend to be the kings of this huge castle. While our parents continued eating, drinking their cider, wine and coffee and after their coffee one last glass of bottled cider, we'd head off to explore the childhood paradise. There were my cousins and young children from the neighbouring farms and we'd climb the wall that surrounded the castle at our secret meeting place and we'd land on the far side, helping each other as we went along, in a clump of high bamboo sticks. The latter, from which we used to cut branches to make fishing rods, the huge fir trees and the pine trees that had been twisted by the wind, constituted our exotic world. We'd pretend to be Japanese, or Chinese. We played war games with rusty old cannons, we'd go on imaginary long journeys in the Berlin coaches, the Landau carriages or else, heading down the park towards the pond, we'd get out the old rowboat.

'Don't ever go too close to the edge of the pond,' mother would warn me. 'Do you see all those trees over there? Well, if you put them all together you would still never reach the bottom of the pond.'

But, of course, all that advice was quickly forgotten when she was out of sight. I could do anything. The young girls could stay on the bank for all I cared, and let out shrieks of admiration or horror. The boys were sailing like the Spanish conquistadors over the murky depths.

Then there was also the castle where we'd have our feasts. There we'd come across onions, dahlias and nuts which were put out to dry on the tiled floor. There was ornate furniture there as well as antique chandeliers.

One afternoon in January we were pretending to say Mass. Outside the chapel you could heard a strong wind blowing in the trees, causing the loose stained-glass windows to bang together. The candles that we had found in a press cast a scary light around the chapel. The others had wanted to play the burial of the Lady of the Château. I, however, wanted to say a Mass for all the martyrs of the Church because I had found a red piece of curtain material that was covering a chandelier. Anyway, I must have conceded to the wishes of the majority because I was dressed in black while officiating at the ceremony.

Just as we were singing the *Dies irae* the door opened. The Lady appeared. A taxi had to have brought her from the train station at Saint-Séveran. We hadn't heard her approaching at all. There she stood, motionless, looking at us through her lorgnette. The girls were too frightened to run away; our singing had stopped dead as if the record had been stopped. The boys took flight as she made her way towards the altar. For my part, hindered as I was by my mock vestments, I stayed where I was – there was no possible escape.

'Out you go, you little brats,' she shouted at the girls. 'As for you, you rascal,' she said to me, 'Come over here.'

My first thought was that I was destined for a stay in the dungeons. How often had we searched in vain for those same dungeons! They were located in the underground passages that linked all the castles of the universe. To my surprise, the Lady's voice suddenly became soft, somewhat solemn, with a tinge of sadness. She was almost friendly in her demeanour and I stole a look at her face which was as beautiful as a face that has been marked by death. It was transparent and yet seemed to be hiding some great secret.

'You were saying Mass?' she asked.

Thankfully she didn't ask for whom the Mass was being said. She seemed distant and yet close at the same time as she stood in front of the pitiful coffin we had erected in the middle of the chapel. I replied 'Yes Madame' with forced acquiescence.

'You have nice honest-looking eyes,' she observed. 'Do you think you might like to become a priest some day?'

I felt as though I was going to win this particular game, that I'd escape the dungeons and get away without having to tell my parents about what had happened. There would be no big scene created at home.

'Oh yes, Madame,' I replied.

How was I going to manage to get around this in confession? I had told a white lie in order to get out of a spot of bother. That was it, that was all I had to say. There would be no need to go into any further detail.

'Follow me, young man,' she said to me. 'Maria! Maria! What are you up to now, you lazy lump?'

Maria, who had come home with her boss, was waiting at the door, fully expecting an outburst of some sort.

'Bring up the cases,' Madame Désesseule ordered her. 'Find me some sweets and a few biscuits for young Sulivan who was saying Mass. Come on then, young man, where do you think you're going? Follow me.'

She took my hand. It was as if I was the heir apparent to all this:

my hand was in this soft warm hand. The others would never believe what had happened to me. I was ready to betray any confidence to make this moment last.

'Over this way,' I said, pushing aside the bamboo sticks. A young girl could be heard crying softly, totally forgotten about by the adults.

'I know, I know. From now on you'll come in this way,' the Lady said to me, showing me towards the door and at the same time giving me biscuits and sweets. Come and see me some time and don't be afraid of me, I don't bite,' she said, passing her hand through my hair.

The following year my uncle and aunt were for some unfathomable reason removed from their position on the farm of the Grand Manoir. I only found out what had happened by overhearing some snippets of my parents' conversation. Madame Désesseule had accused them of stealing wood. The case went to court.

A lawyer from Rennes had come down to the trial. 'Look at this man,' he said to the judges, 'this stupid man who cannot control his drinking, this lazy good-for-nothing, how are we to believe him when he says that he didn't steal the wood?' My poor uncle, who was a moderate drinker and as honest as the day is long, hadn't a hope. How was he going to explain in front of these learned gentlemen from the city, who didn't know him, who didn't want to find out anything about him that wasn't included in their impersonal files? He started to cry; his tears were obviously seen as being an admission of guilt. A short time afterwards we discovered the real reason for this eviction. Madame Désesseule, rather than go to the bother of repairing what was in effect a crumbling concern, was renting out the farm to another farmer and bulldozing the outhouses.

For obvious reasons I never set foot in that house again.

Mother had to force me to go to school. She hit me with a stick she'd picked up from among the firewood and dragged me off screaming. At the first break I fled to the forest. I was discovered and surrounded like a hunted animal. I believe I made the transition from childlike innocence, with its perfect natural understanding, to the world of words and thoughts, with a kind of obscure unease. I certainly don't regret this transition: I would in no way wish to appear that foolish. Life is like moving from one confused piece of knowledge to the next. On the way you are constantly being tempted by art and literature as well as by the development of a clear way of thinking which you fearfully build up in an attempt to protect yourself against suffering. I always seemed to be torn in many different directions: this might have been the legacy of the innocence of that stubborn child who hid in the forest, who would often choose Dionysius over Apollo, Jerusalem over Athens, who would prefer Meister Eckhart and John of the Cross to Thomas Aquinas, Malebranche to Spinoza, India to Greece, who would later bring the Bible with him wherever he went, the *Elegies of Duino, Plexus*, and finally *Voyage to the End of the Night*. This same person would willingly swap many of the classical poets for the work of Whitman.

I now see that as a child I was perfectly in communion with the earth. I loved the rain, the sun and the cold in equal measure and I never knew if I was really happy. By just becoming aware of happiness you are already separating yourself from it in a way. The world is not a major spectacle for the child: he is very much a part of everything that is happening. People attempt to force him to leave this stage behind him and to make him into a enlightened little animal who will help turn the wheel of the huge social machine. Adults surround him, bend over him: whenever he repeats the conventional formulae, they applaud him.

'You'll have to become like us as quickly as possible,' they say. 'Learn what everybody else already knows, have the feelings that you should be experiencing, the fears. Leave behind for ever that most fragile and secret part that is hidden deep within you.'

I have had a long and hard struggle against words. During catechism class in school the priest told us that mortal sin could be likened to a squirrel that a child picked up on his way to school. During class the squirrel started eating into his chest. It was the same with mortal sin. Despite this explanation, I could never remember mortal sin having that particular effect on me. I must have been irreparably hardened against sin.

Every Friday we were forced to do the Stations of the Cross. The priest asked us to shed 'rivers of tears, day and night'. He'd finish with the following little ditty; 'And let us die for Him as He laid down His life for us.' I knew this priest well; he was a nice sort, paternal and with

45

a love of fishing and cards. He used to carry in his pocket a small white box that would shine in the light when he took it out from under his cassock, still warm from the contact with his body. He'd never stop asking us questions. They were all very simple, such as: Is the Virgin Mary the Mother of God? Is God all-powerful? How many times, listening to priests talking thus to children, have I remembered the taste in my mouth of the warm almond sweets we got from the priest's box during catechism class! The purpose of the priests' words, like the sweets, was to encourage the right reflexes. Why did God let His faithful die if He was as powerful as all that? When I would later discover that God was also poor and meek of spirit, I was absolutely thrilled. But in primary school everything was neatly explained, no questions were invited. You put into the magic hat what you wanted to take out of it. How do people lose the faith? You don't have to look any further than the way catechism is taught to find the reason. At the time I was only interested in my almond sweet that the nice priest would take out of his white tin and put in our mouths with a little tap on the cheek.

Father Motel had a big fat belly, which wasn't very well supported by the frayed belt with tassels that he wore. For all his talk, I never actually saw *him* crying during the Stations of the Cross. He didn't look at all like someone who wanted to die for Our Lord. As for the little problems I mentioned having with words, like the vast majority of men, Father Motel never talked seriously about their import at all. His teeth had yellow nicotine stains on them. Maybe one shouldn't talk about the love of God with nicotine-stained teeth.

If somebody says the word 'table' to me I know what they mean. The word 'love' on the other hand would cause me a lot more difficulty, and as for 'God' . . . I'm less fascinated by the word itself as by the tone, the gesture, the look people use when saying it. *The truth is not like a minted coin that you can choose to bank or to spend.* How often have these words of the German philosopher, Hegel, come back to haunt me. The child comes into contact with this world through his ability to make reasoned calculations and through his ability to speak. When it comes to the question of faith, however, there is the danger that the child's receptiveness will be used to begin a process of conditioning. The clarity that is conveyed through a grouping of words and a line of reasoning can be accessible to everyone and to no one at the same time. It can fall into the trap of theorising. Christians have long since forgotten that it is lack of faith that is natural and commonplace: there can be a danger involved in presenting the supernatural in a way that would lead one to believe that it is straightforward and logical. It is probably effective for the Christian world to put forward in the short term and in certain specific circumstances a technical vocabulary. You reach a large number of people in this way and thus create an artificial sort of unity. This very quickly develops into a jargon. In the verb 'communiquer' there is *commun*, which means common. It is not a common or a shared knowledge that can be conveyed in this instance. Christian knowledge is more of an art than a technique. It is terribly dangerous to reach knowledge too quickly; to think that you know what there is to be known. Adults tend to gauge how advanced children are by the vocabulary they use. In this order of things knowledge can only go from what is vague to what is clear. It is not through logical reasoning that one comes to terms with mystery. When you seek to attract a large public you are, in a manipulative way and under the guise of altruism, substituting what is essentially an advertising technique for the true message of Scripture. Certainly, for a short time you have a number of people in your power, but it doesn't last long. When the particular set of sociological circumstances that brought together certain pressures disappears, so also will any sense of loyalty that the people may have been feeling. The parable, on the other hand, works in a simpler way by using a poetic language that is unadorned and simple. Maybe this language will only touch the hearts of the few, but it is often the few that influence the masses. The itinerary proposed by the Gospel is long and difficult because it works on the consciousness first before moving on to the reflexes. When people stop mixing up conditioning and education, and more especially culture and the process of evangelisation, we will have gone a long way towards producing a new vision of humankind.

Many men who have been moulded in a very narrow way are said to be like prostitutes who get married and who allow themselves to be treated like objects who are bereft of the capacity for human love and affection. The man who enters into such a contract will have to be extremely patient indeed and to invest years of uncertain trust in his partner without any obvious reciprocation. Then maybe one day from the seed of genuine love will spring the miracle of a true partnership, a communion. Thus it is that so many men and women who have been cheated on, with or without their knowledge, who submitted to all the laws governing relationships, are for a long period, or maybe even definitively, incapable of entering into any spontaneous inner pact with their partner for having so long confused their inner truth with reflexes that are not even their own.

We were told that you *must* feel sorry. It wasn't as simple as that. Genuine repentance is not a categorical imperative and does not relate to any specific commandment, since it is God Himself who gives us the wherewithal to repent. Anyway, I finally reached the stage where I no longer said, 'I'm sorry, really sorry.' It was a waste of time for me to try to feel this emotion. Eventually I started to feel sorry before I had even committed a sin. Mother used to say 'You worry too much about words. You should just do what you are told. Remember, the Church knows more about these things than you will ever know.'

There was something wrong. If you listened to the religious experts you'd spend all your time considering in minute detail all those tiny problems that sometimes invade your conscience; you'd keep on making sacrifices, praying, doing good deeds. All of which would prevent you from living your life to the full. Life wasn't meant to be taken that seriously, I can see that now. Because they saw the danger that people would ignore a lot of what they said, these experts tended to exaggerate the advice they gave in an attempt to reach some sort of happy medium. I have the impression that many of my friends, who are indeed among the closest I have, rejected this burden that had weighed them down for many years simply in order to maintain their mental health. That temptation would also secretly assail me for a time. However, this is not the time to speak about that particular subject and in any case it's my mother who is supposed to be the subject of my deliberations in this book.

One day when my mother had gone to the market, no doubt with the idea of sniffing out a few sweet things for us to eat, on pushing open the door to her bedroom (this room was full of marvels with its flowery curtains and its mirrored wardrobes, its chest of drawers full of the most unbelievable treasures) I came across the vision of our maid, Lucie, who was looking at her naked body in the mirror. The only feeling I can remember having at this wonderful sight was one of peaceful amazement. The sight of this naked body gave me the same pleasure as looking at the trees and the animals. It was explained to me later in life that some images could lead to sin. Maybe I took it up wrongly. In any case I know that I often accused myself of that particular sin without having the slightest idea why it was sinful. When images or pictures started to form within me I felt guilty at first, then afraid. I often had to run off to the church to confess my sins. Crazy, wasn't I? I'm not sure if all children are scrupulous the way I was. The truth of the matter is that I took everything that was said to me literally. It must be supremely dangerous, under the pretext that you are trying to inculcate a sense of sin in him, to use a child's natural fearfulness, his gullibility. Fear takes over and he becomes incapable of making any real moral judgement.

Lucie had an unfortunate time of it. It seems that she liked to go off with boys after the music lessons that were organised in the parish hall for young people. A few played the clarinet, but that's not important. She became pregnant and many years later I would find out that mother had wanted to take her back into the house after the birth of the baby. And this was the act of a woman who people would have you believe was a Jansenist! I think that the only sin she was really frightened of was the sin of rejecting one's faith. She had only kind words to say about the local people who were known to be a bit wild.

I read her a page from Raïssa Maritain one day, which stated that the life story of each individual could summarise the entire biblical story of humanity. It continued by remarking that, just as in the Bible you had the stage of instinct, then that of the law followed by freedom and grace, so too today there were men governed by instinct who live, so to speak, outside the realm of the law, then there are the men of the law who are strangers to the idea of freedom of choice and action, and finally there are the men of grace. In fact, each one of us could only be judged according to his or her own enlightenment. Her reaction was that it was funny how a simple peasant woman like herself had always known that to have been the case.

Images that are connected with words keep coming back to me. Father Motel used to say to us in catechism class, 'Can you all hear my watch?' We could all hear it in the deathly silence. He must have done something to that watch to get it to tick so loudly. 'Well then', he'd say to us, 'What is my watch saying to us? Forever, never, in Hell forever, in Heaven forever.' In Father Motel's scheme of things, hearing about what is was like to physically burn in Hell was nothing compared to what you suffered when you were damned, that is, deprived for all eternity of the possibility of seeing God. That was the worst thing of all. Personally, I didn't mind not being able to see God. There were so many extraordinary things that one never got to see: the Niagara Falls, a red partridge, a stoat with a spotted coat, for example. In truth, I feel that I have always thought in the same way – you can't make God into some sort of object that you observe. This doesn't even come close to the divine reality. I'm not in the least bit surprised that Lazarus said nothing when he came back from the dead. He had seen nothing concrete. No more than the child in the throes of happiness has any chance of describing what he is feeling.

One Sunday, as mother was recounting things that had happened to her, I began to remember a few memories of my own. We were talking about our big meadow, which we called Séléhem, when a face came into my mind. What was his name? He used to have a red bike that he wasn't shy about showing off. One day the teacher was asking him some questions on his catechism:

'Where was he born?'

'In Séléhem,' he answered, 'in a poor star!'

I wouldn't boast about my own knowledge of these same issues at that time. When, at the end of the Our Father, I heard: *Libera nos a malo* I thought of Saint-Malo and the sea.

Our friend had another great victory and this one would become famous. The Archbishop, who was visiting the parish, decided to give us a grilling on our knowledge of the catechism.

'Who am I?' he asked

Nobody could come up with an answer.

'Look at me carefully,' he said.

And, with these words, he took out the little purple hat that bishops wear during religious ceremonies and twirled it on the top of his index finger. He then pulled up his cassock to reveal his purple socks. Finally he flashed his bishop's ring at us. Suddenly, a quiet voice could be heard at the back of the class.

'You're a show-off, mister, that's what you are!'

A few months after that, the same boy had a fatal accident while riding his red bicycle. I wonder was it he also who gave the amusing answer to the question: 'What were Our Lord's last words on the Cross?'

'I couldn't give a damn,' the boy replied, 'because I'm going to rise again on the third day.'

For my First Communion I tried to imitate energetically the feelings we were supposed to have. I was the best in the class at catechism. It's strange but I don't think I was in any way proud of that achievement. Vanity would come later in life. I was obliged to come first in a sense. After all, mother had bought me a big catechism with explanations of the different points written into it. Not only did I have to reel off the catechism, but also the explanations. Coming first in my mother's eyes had to be proof of divine providence. In the villages around where we lived, Holy Communion was treated something like a competition. Two days after the result was announced my teacher asked me to stay behind for a minute after class was over.

'You look unhappy, child,' he said.

I tried to explain to him what was up and, being unable to find any satisfactory means of doing so, I stupidly muttered something like, 'I don't think I have found God, sir.' He didn't laugh at this outburst, of that I am sure. He remained silent for a long time then he cleared his throat and I thought I saw tears in his eyes when he said, 'That generally doesn't stop too many people from sleeping at night, you know.'

He took my hand and became very serious. I think he was talking for his own benefit as much, if not more, than for mine. When I think back on this incident now I almost want to cry. I didn't understand what he was saying then but I think I have a good idea of the words he used.

'God is never easy to come to grips with, child,' he said. 'You have to prefer Him to your own vanity, to money, to everyone else, even His

51

priests and ministers. When you have undergone a period of suffering, you will have Him with you forever.'

He walked me towards the door and with his back half-turned to me, he said, 'Watch how you go on this one, Sulivan. Don't let anyone take you in.'

I can see now why mother was pushing me in this way. She wanted to enclose me in a world of habit, which for her was very close to the eternal plan. How could I be surprised by this attitude? The priests at this time tended to preach about laws and obligations. In this way they had succeeded in transforming Christianity into something approaching a natural religion. In their eyes the rural order in which the Church still played a dominant role was an expression of the divine will. They had forgotten about freedom, without which there is no real faith. I find it strange that it has taken so long for this truth to be proclaimed in a solemn manner. If the Church had taken the concept of freedom seriously, the changes in the world would not have threatened Christianity in any way. The only thing that would have come under pressure was that which was no longer valid, having been linked to a past when power and prestige were the dominant features of the institutional Church. Many of those who refuse the truth are really refusing falsified truths, which undermine a person's conscience.

I see a child; I think it's myself; he is running on a road that leads to the forest. He's back in the forest. Why is the boy coming back? Everything is enveloped in a fog. I know that mother is getting married today. I must be feeling shame, fear and emptiness. When I look back on it now, I feel nothing. But I know that for years I carried a deep scar inside me, a scar that wouldn't leave me and to which I couldn't even give a name. Animals must feel like that when they are seized upon by a panic that cannot be expressed in thoughts or words. The child is wearing his sailor suit, which he always has to wear on special occasions. Having come out of the forest, he stands motionless at the point where the different paths converge. He tries to listen to the noises, the laughs that filter through from Fontaines noires. Someone runs up to me and I take flight again. No good; he catches up with me. 'Listen here, young man, do you want to kill your mother or what? You didn't even attend the church service.' I see mother getting up from the table when she sees my captor and myself arriving. Her face, which is filled with sadness, approaches me in a haze.

Initially I was of the opinion that my natural antipathy to parties and my horror of ceremonies was the result of my mother's remarriage. That was something of an overstatement. Our likes and dislikes have very deep roots. You start off believing that they are due to specific judgements and choices you have made up until the time when you admit to yourself that it is probably a case of your being too bored or too lazy to change your ways. Eventually you see that you are simply incapable of staying put. Deep down I have been happy to refer to my inability to conform to the social niceties as the offshoot of a value judgement I have made about their futility. In fact, it's just a case of my being basically intolerant. For the most part, if I think I am being consistent in this area it's because I have nothing to lose or nothing to gain. I have seen former friends of mine reluctantly entering into these social games because their line of work demanded that they do so. As time goes by they begin to like the artificiality for its own sake, because of the ritual that is attached to it. But in the end, who is left to nod approvingly at what they have achieved? They might be the President of a company or maybe even a Monsignor. But if they were stripped of all their external decorations how would you know they were Presidents or Monsignors? This is why there are so many mutual-admiration societies; they allow people who only rely on appearances to keep afloat.

My mother always told me not to be so critical about the major religious ceremonies. She herself always had a liking for spectacular rituals. They weren't just an alibi for her.

I was never able to call my mother's second husband, 'father'. I don't really know why that was the case. It caused me some degree of unease because I have to say that he was a genuinely good man. I don't think that my mother ever really loved him deeply. She respected him and wouldn't hear a bad word said against him by anyone. After all, she had been united to him in the holy sacrament of matrimony and in addition he was the father of her two children. Incidentally I had no bother looking on as the latter as my brothers, at least when, having gone through the phase when I exerted a tyrannical control over them, they were old enough to be my friends. I know that she had gone ahead with this marriage against the better judgement of her family who thought she could have done better. There are petty snobberies even among the poor. He was a simple man who also had nostalgic memories of the war and it never ceased to amaze him that he was finally responsible for running a farm. He referred to mother as *la Patronne* (the Boss).

At meal times she liked to talk about my father. 'Your father', she'd start up turning towards me. I used to turn away, or change the subject or just leave the room. I never knew whether this was done out of a feeling of solidarity towards my real father, who, I believed, would have wanted us to stay quiet on this subject, or whether I was siding with this new father for whom I felt this whole topic must have been a terrible humiliation. I never saw him betray the slightest emotion at any stage during these discussions. Men who spend their time tilling the land are uncomplicated; they may be hurt but so deep-down that they cannot find words to express what they are feeling. Or maybe they just know instinctively how to avoid having worthless feelings, how to dispense with artificial moral dilemmas.

Soon the time came for me to make a choice about my education: I could go to the state-run school or enter the minor seminary. My uncle, the soldier priest I have already described, taught in the Catholic school. I was very frightened of him and his fanaticism. I opted for the minor seminary because I thought he would have less opportunity of watching over me in that particular environment. I have to say that mother was happy with my decision. Another deciding factor was how pleasant all the priests were with me, how attentive they were to my needs, what nice things they said! I had no reason to disappoint them. What I thought a little strange was the way they adopted a different tone of voice when talking to one another. It wouldn't have bothered me in the slightest if I had been left on holidays permanently with nothing to do other than to mind the animals. As I have already said, the present moment was my sole preoccupation. This is not to say that I was not touched by certain books I read or sermons I heard. I put everything into the same basket: Mathias Sandorf, Louis de Gonzague and Michel Strogoff, the curé d'Ars and Father Damien, nobility of spirit and sanctity. I always came to the rescue of Tarcisius whenever I felt him to be in any danger. I felt at one with Francis of Assisi; I could imagine us being showered with blows and dragged through the mire. This was what perfect joy was about. I imagined what it would have been like had Jesus made the decision to mobilise his legions of angels; the Roman soldiers would have run away, terrified. Or if he had spat abuse at the crowd of spectators and the soldiers while nailed to the cross, with his halo shining above the crown of thorns. 'My poor misguided children', he would say and he would get down calmly from the cross while those who had been looking wide-eyed at the side of the road fell to their knees in adoration. The only problem with my imaginary scenario was that it would all have to start over again since Jesus had to die eventually anyway.

Was it this desire I've always had to take risks that inspired my decision to enter the priesthood? Or maybe it was the contempt I had for ordinary jobs? When I was taken away from the trees, the animals, I thought life was strangely flat, meaningless. Who taught me the void that is at the heart of existence? Is it possible that I read it in my mother's eyes? Had I been too attentive to the pious sermons of the priests, which didn't worry either the adults or the person giving them but which penetrated a child's heart? It is possible that, as I had so little importance in other people's eyes and no other real object to wish for, I grabbed on to God as others march behind a flag. In order to be left in peace I gave in to the words and the looks that were assailing me from all sides. I gave adults the answers they wished to hear. I was going to start living as a serious person does, take my rightful place in society, stand tall. There could be no doubt that God conveyed prestige on you, put you up on a pedestal. I saw everything through the eyes of Sirius, a star in the firmament. I have a metaphysical soul. It can make you very happy sometimes to be different, to drop whatever it is you are doing. When you have been uprooted from the earth, you seek the refuge of God's love in the same way as one hides away in a tower.

The minor seminary was a purgatory. 'All you who enter here must stop being yourselves. You'll have to imitate others, only exist in order to please your teachers, say goodbye to friendship.' People told us too often in the seminary that we were the elect, the privileged ones, that we had a vocation to become saints. It was true. At the same time, the priesthood then offered unbelievable opportunities for a simple peasant such as myself who had nothing and who was being asked to reign over an abstract and somehow unreal world. All someone like this wanted was to believe in his own innate superiority. They should have gone at it somewhat more slowly. Our teachers thought they were detaching us from the outside world, opening us out to God's pure love. They were also feeding our pride, that most terrible unmentionable pride that goes so far as to use God Himself.

Later I would throw myself passionately into the study of theology. I immersed myself in things spiritual in the same way as others throw themselves into art, literature, mathematics. I was well-placed to deceive others as to my real feelings about theology, but I was kidding myself first and foremost. When you occupy a slightly marginal position you can get as enthusiastic as you like, that's where the problem lies. For example you can love humanity, the Mystical Body, all the more if you are removed from the mass of mankind. You can be as sincere and as self-assured as you like, you still have to discover to your sorrow that love is an abstract concept, that our theories about the phenomenon that is God remain hopelessly scholarly.

Far too few teachers know that you can excel in theology, in spiritual life, even in piety, and still have a heart that is completely hard. I have seen a lot of pious and clever men die at an advanced age, never having woken up to reality. Likewise, I have seen efficient and famous apostles strut about without knowing that their hearts were empty. They were taken up with so many different thoughts, busy blocking up any holes through which real life might enter and touch their hearts. They were part of a milieu for whom appearances are all that matters. I think I know what I'm talking about when I mention the hibernation of the heart. Don't make any mistake about it – when you try to do away with freedom from the beginning, you will only be left with a small fraction of it at the end of the day. This will explain clearly why it is that intelligent, rich and loyal people live sterile lives – they are only heard to a certain extent by those who live by the same set of illusory rules.

In pretending to develop Christian or moral responsibility in the child we are being somewhat premature. We teach him how to imitate the hypocritical reflexes of an adult who is often more driven by fear and social conventions than by love. The child is put kneeling down and he is burdened with loads that are too heavy for him to carry. The adults, who don't have the same amount of baggage to carry, say that he should be proud and full of joy. One day will come the realisation that he has been taken in, that is, unless he holds on desperately to this value system which has been inculcated into him and which is inflexible and sick.

I confess unashamedly that I allowed my soul to be contaminated by perfectly sincere and good people for whom I had great respect. I was part of the process myself to the extent that I was anxious to preserve my smooth existence and frightened of being left out in the cold. I admit also that I confused Christian culture with the message of the Gospel. But I thank God that I came at a crossroads, which left behind a naturalised sort of Christian culture, where all that counted were power and prestige. In the future, awaiting birth even though it had been born for thousands of years, there was the new Christian order, more humble and truthful than what had gone before.

For a long time now I have been wondering about what my exact reasons were for doing the things I have done. Why is it that I always try to find the answers in my past? A person has a whole lifetime in which to make decisions. A vocation is always there waiting for you.

I think it strange to imagine now that mother was present at my First Communion and at my ordination but I have no memory of her being there. She must have been at the ceremony, dressed up in all her finery like everyone else, a part of the overall decor. The celebrations associated with these occasions didn't interest me at all. In truth I will never know how one could have made such a shameful spectacle out of events that should in essence be very private. During these ceremonies it probably struck me that mother was looking at me through other people's eyes. She wasn't seeing me up there on the altar but the conventional image of the priest that we probably all need to see to be reassured that everything is as it should be. I would so like to have shared the secret with her but how does one set about explaining things of this nature? I felt guilty at my inability to experience the normal feelings people have on such matters.

I have the impression that the man who returns now every Sunday to see his mother has found again a part of his childhood. A significant period of his life has gone by. He did as he was told during this time: he studied, taught, helped people in his own awkward way, but, above all, talked to them. He set up one activity, then moved on to a new project. In order to stand his ground, when faced with experts in morality and in orthodoxy, who are in fact totally inept and who are the mouthpieces of public opinion, he had to have some notables on his side. What pride he felt for a while at the thought of being supported by these esteemed people! When the 'respectable' lobby were attacking you for some reason it was simply necessary to elicit the support of other people who really didn't share the prejudices of the former group. This was diplomacy at its best. You can feel a genuine sense of pleasure at juggling, pulling different strings, to ensure that things turn out the way you want them to. What an effort I made to conform to the traditional image people had of the priest. It was no use, I would always feel that I was merely acting like a civil servant. Because I didn't have the courage to announce or live out the paradoxes of the Gospel, having neither enough pride nor faith to plan on being a martyr, I bought into the whole religious culture thing. Being naturally unable to be totally hypocritical, too cowardly to receive real blows, I found my niche – culture. It saves a person while allowing him to stay on the surface of things. I could present dogma in a modern form, quote from the specialists, hide behind the popes' pronouncements, explore literature and the new world of cinema in order to find the correct symbols, the lessons learnt by others. I would preserve the illusion for a while in this manner.

Sometimes I came out with some fearful truths, or ones that I considered such, or which were received as such, but which in reality were commonly accepted as truths by everybody because of the way they had been put forward over the years by others. As I was finishing up my sermon, I'd put everything back in place, reassuring the people by balancing truth in the name of a higher wisdom, while wanting to forget all the time that I was just protecting myself and my own beliefs in this way. I was good at this sort of thing. People would congratulate me. I was told I was daring, that I had a well-balanced view of things. It was more a question of being clever. The women in particular were ecstatic about my performance, and then there was, of course, the small pocket of men and women who, in a large town or city, do the rounds of all the conferences and seminars. Was I being dishonest in all this? In my own way I suppose I was handing out almond sweets like Father Motel.

What brought about my downfall or saved me, depending on how you look at it, was this: when I was congratulated for having spoken so beautifully, while I felt the usual sense of pride, I would also feel great sadness, followed by irritation. I could never forget the inherent contradiction in the idea that you can announce the message of the Gospel while at the same time making a career out of it. I couldn't see Christianity through the eyes of an unbeliever or through those of a self-assured believer: that sort of Christianity struck me as being a set of rituals and speeches. Men dressed up in theatrical costumes waxing on about suitable themes. Those who were believers were like members of a club, a mutual respect society who had a special pass to get into heaven. They would never stop being mere spectators. They would never be active participants. A leader would say: 'Come on now, you're going to have to participate.' But mere visual participation in a world that is steeped in spectacles of all sorts was becoming more and more insignificant. What has taking a meal together have to do with spectators? When you have a meal with your family and friends, that is not first and foremost a ceremony. Will the symbolic sign one day cease to hide what it should seek to signify?

How was I to avoid becoming a professional, that was the question I constantly asked myself. How was I meant to escape the trap of repeating the same old formulae? Repetition should involve renewal, a deeper awareness of things, but more often than not it is merely a means of reproducing what others have said. The teacher, faced with conveying a technique to his students, would probably confront the same dilemma, but when he invites them to participate, everything disintegrates into bedlam. We live in the age of the lecturer and the preacher who are capable of saying sensible things on every subject under the sun; or maybe we are living under the dictatorship of the newsreader who merely says what has been prepared by others. These people speak at fixed times and do so to earn a living. How can we expect them to do otherwise?

Sometimes a prophet emerges from their number. Instead of seeking out external symmetry, the prophet tries to attain complicity with his listeners in the deepest recesses of their souls. To achieve this, he first of all has to break open doors and windows, the shells people use to protect themselves; he has to make them blind so that they can be taught to see differently. The Lord says: *Look, I am putting words in your mouth for you to pull things out by their roots and knock them down, so that you can then build and plant anew.* But whenever a person speaks in a passionate way he is forced to hold his tongue. How little things have changed since the time of Amos, the shepherd from Teqoa. The other way they deal with the prophet is to placate him by showering him with honours and prestige.

But how could the person I have been talking about have dared to opt for martyrdom when he saw how dull and hum-drum his existence was? What's more he had no desire to further his career. He kept on discussing in public, polishing up his act, seeking to be cultivated. He reached the point where he admired those who said nothing or those who stuck to banalities, being deliberately watchful. In a sense they were being more honest than he. They were tricking people less than those who, like himself, knew how to play the right tune, comment intelligently on things, come out for or against.

Sometimes a memory comes back to me; I am at a meeting for those belonging to the 'middle classes', as it was put. They were there to discuss the Epistle to the Philippians. Saint Paul speaks as though he were enclosed in a prison cell: *I have willingly lost everything, I consider material objects to be worthless. I no longer know what justice means in my own particular case. I prefer to push ahead and forget about what I am leaving behind.*

'In the light of this letter written to the Philippians, what does a Christian existence mean for you?' The group leader's question fails to elicit any response. We read over a few passages for the second time.

Then suddenly a timid voice speaks about persecution, joy, the primacy of love, which can overcome all prejudice. It goes on to mention the blacks and the whites, equality among all men. People start squirming in their seats, this isn't the sort of thing they are used to hearing – they feel uncomfortable. There is silence. A quarter of an hour later, however, the room is alive; everyone is speaking in an animated manner. What has happened? The group have found a means of short-circuiting the discussion by getting back to more familiar terrain – Solemn Communion, the very important question of whether one should wear a white alb or ordinary clothes, armbands. Then there is the debate about public or parochial education. The middle classes have no wish whatsoever to hear Saint Paul say that Christian life is all about taking risks, that it needs to be freed from all the Jewish influences of the time and the new ones that assail us today. Equally they don't want to know anyone's opinion on breaking down social barriers, or about how Christianity is much more important than daily happenings or even death. A phrase of Sartre keeps on returning to my head like a tune: *People are engaged in conversation; something explosive is going to happen that will light up the dark recesses of a soul and then everybody will feel his own inner self coming alive. But no, the danger has passed, and people start exchanging the same worthless badinage as before.*

Religious babble is the same thing as the mundane drivel that is spoken in some circles. The Councils of the Church, rumours that emanate from certain corridors of power, the new and the old priests, Michel de Saint-Pierre, are you for him or against him, the Mass in French or Latin, where do you stand on this? Everything is turned into an object. In this way, people become insulated against the real burning truths. I know this priest, my brother, my soulmate in so many ways, who wondered one Saturday night what he was going to say the following day. Because you have to say something during the sermon, after all. He thinks about it after watching the telly, or after his bridge party. *The kingdom of God is like a merchant who was looking for precious pearls.* The kingdom? What interpretation would be given of this word? Better check up the dictionary of biblical theology, or see what our friend Father de la Tour has to say about it. After typing out a few phrases, auto-pilot takes over. After all, he's been giving sermons for years. On Sunday morning he gets very animated; he talks about giving everything up, how there is no room for selfishness. Then he concludes with a familiar little tune – they would have to make a greater effort, pray more. 'You were brilliant, absolutely brilliant, Father!' He must have got carried away. That's called over-compensating. But love, when it is lived in the heart of the poor person, may set fire to anything. When a sincere man, touched by the sermon, comes to ask him after the ceremony, 'What do you think I should do?' the priest is in a right quandary. He had not reckoned on some poor fellow having the idea of starting afresh, living in a more authentic manner. All he can think to say is, 'Take it easy, my good man' and recommends that he take some Valium tablets and go and see his analyst. Allow me to laugh at the good of this. *A Magus appeared one day in a platform that had been raised up in the air, and spoke for a long time about vice and virtue. This wise man divided into several parts what had no need to be divided; he proved to people everything that was clear, taught them everything that they already knew. He spoke with passion, but it was controlled passion.* There can be no doubt that Voltaire listened to sermons. Woe be to the person who announces the truth without having come to terms with it himself. Or else you have the option of allowing yourself to be judged in the light of that same truth. On the other hand, by changing the truth of the Gospel into an academic discourse, you are in danger of propagating a subtle lie, which can be indiscernible to your audience.

For a long time he had consoled himself by saying that the Church had always accommodated appearances and flowery speeches because it had been necessary to appeal to the masses at their level. But then again there were also the saints and the mystics. A good mixture was a healthy thing, they maintained. It was no longer possible to believe this. It was now clear that far from leading to the heart of reality, the world of appearances was keeping people eternally on the outside and that it was preventing the non-believer from even paying attention to what lay behind the appearances. The Gospel never said 'If you love the public display, you will save the masses'. The Gospel was never preoccupied with numbers. By that do I mean that it seeks to save an elite at the expense of the majority? Not really; I am merely stating the message of the Gospel which says that the leaven is the most important, that it alone will give life and energy to the Church. I tend to believe that the eternal truth has not chosen to reach man through his reflexes but to pass from one soul that has become enflamed to another. Any truth that has not known some human warmth is a false truth. Jesus rejected all worldly temptations in the desert.

So this priest we've been talking about continued rattling on about things and organising different events. Avarice and the gift of giving yourself to others are more closely linked than you might think. His generosity was just a desperate attempt to forget a few basic truths he thought he had found, not only in Scripture but in the whole history of the Church. Because there are some truths that, although largely put aside by Christendom, were always emphasised by the doctors and a number of the Church's theologians as being the essential truths and which called into question a number of its attitudes. Our young priest felt he had moved far away from the Church but that he was coming closer to his heart's desire. At no time did he ever think of calling into question the fundamental truths connected with faith, nor their doctrinal expression for that matter. He believed, however, that you needed to divest yourself of all certitude in order for the real message of the Gospel message to enter your heart. However, it was more complex than that. Among a number of theologians and philosophers alike, as on the conscious level of some Christians, doctrinal constructions, in their effort to tie everything up in a neat bundle and present a totality, could be grasped or at least used in total good faith, like a natural system that seeks to find a cure for our anxiety. The message itself became almost natural. A fanatical type of religion, which ought to make revelations accessible, could actually hide them and, in a way, prevent people from seeing the reality. It could put forward, for example, the idea that Jesus' lot was to be abandoned and alone in death, that this doesn't just happen in a historical sense but in our day-to-day lives, that we need to break free from the world of convictions, from the consolations of religion itself, in order to find ourselves face to face with divine poverty.

The fabulous efforts of the rationalist philosophers who sought in a thousand different ways to bring the particular back to the general, to strip pain and even death of their sting and the protest they evoke, by arranging them in a totality and by choosing to lean more and more on necessity, he found again, in a spontaneous manner, in the minds that religion had taken hold of. This attempt had the merit certainly of ensuring a cure to religious ills and evoking a sense of protection – in brief, it helped people to live. Its very essence was directed towards Christ who had died and risen from the dead. But in a devious way people could slip into this mind-set and stand apart from other human beings. It was impossible, without being dishonest, to blame modern thinkers for this dilemma: they were instinctively moving away from religion and from religious people because they suspected an exagerration and selfishness in certain religious attitudes.

How happy our priest had been when his whole life was contained in a narrow thought system. He had answers to all the questions and was amazed that nobody would listen to him, so rigorous was his logic. Divine love was just a weapon in his hands. He was the servant of a religion that was too focused on itself and he didn't even know it. There came a day, therefore, when his wounds caused him to experience the pain of the cross. An impulsive reaction made him run to his mother for help. He knelt in front of her as if he were going to confession. He can see her face still – patient, almost indifferent. Doubtless, only the experience of the love of God can give you some idea of this indifference, which is at once active and passionate. He hadn't even the satisfaction of being able to claim that he had maintained this faith for noble reasons. He wondered if the fear of inflicting his suffering on others wasn't the deciding factor. What he would once have referred to as cowardice he would now call grace. When life breaks you it is not the comfortable image of God we have constructed for ourselves that we seek, but the poor Son of Man who cries out for help within us. It had taken all this life of feigned fervour, of a loyalty that was partly false, of feelings that beset him when he fell victim to suffering; it had required that he forget what he thought he knew, the certitudes that he used as arms against the truth, his convictions that were like shields, in order for him to begin to pray with a more authentic heart, the same prayer but said in a new and different way. He began to hesitate before speaking, he stayed silent, understanding now that other people's sins were also his, other people's disbelief his own disbelief. He saw that the vow of chastity was convenient for someone wishing to foster a comfortable selfishness, that he was taking revenge on his own virtue by despising in too virulent a fashion the world of leisure and sinfulness. For far too long he had thought that celibacy was a virtue in itself. That is a proposition that is in need of qualification. Chastity is a battle that has to be waged, less to protect yourself from others than to be able to give yourself more fully to them. The idea of being beyond reproach was all that was left if renouncing the flesh didn't entail fostering a more loving attitude. All these wounds, which by the grace of God were not incurable, had been necessary for him to be able to discover in reality what he thought he knew how to express in words. Innocence knows more than evil about how to change the way you look on the world, about how to be cured of fear and how to see in the Holy Catholic and apostolic Church of Rome the poor and saintly mother who waits for you and puts up with all your agony.

One day he just could not talk, comment on things, exhort others. If, for example, he had to give a serious talk on some aspect of religion, the previous night he would dream that he was there in front of a crowd, unable to utter a single word. He would hear the sound of running footsteps in the arches of the empty cathedral. Then the sound of footsteps would turn into peals of laughter. He had had enough.

And if I write these things now in fear and trembling, it is not in order to edify, nor to cause scandal, nor to defend my ideas. I am simply trying to describe what was and is an integral part of my consciousness. Far from trying to paint an exemplary picture of myself, I am simply wondering aloud if my temperament, my illusions, are not sufficient to explain everything. And yet the thought comes to me that the obstacles on which I stumbled are also those that prevent many abandoned men of our time from advancing in inner knowledge. I am not baring my soul to you simply in order to explain what new ties now bind me to my mother but perhaps in the very secret hope that I will meet soulmates who are scattered on other roads.

During all the time that had passed until I arrived at the moment of truth, mother had been absent from me. I was fearful for her; she was like a tree on the side of a hill under whose shade you like to rest. The pained tenderness of a mother often demands that you lie or stay silent. The day that she looks on you with genuine friendship, in all your decrepit truth, you are capable of another love.

I began writing to capture that truth that belonged to me, but that wasn't perhaps only mine. Not that I was denying any of the truth that I had learned, and that I had awkwardly attempted to communicate to others, but I sought to find it now in life itself.

The man who every Sunday morning now, after saying Mass for a few friends in a chapel that is no bigger than a pocket handkerchief, comes back home to see his mother, notes the tall square tower of the village, drives along the valley of Jehoshophat, heaves a sigh of relief on seeing the fragile silhouette of his mother at the curtains of the French-window, is the same man who thinks he has now re-discovered something of the truth of childhood.

The bells that used to ring out to announce funerals and baptisms have fallen silent. Mother is seated at the table, her back is turned to the window. The forsythia is always the first to flower. Its flowers appear even before its leaves. The tulips appear, the hyacinths, the soft leaves of the Judas tree, with its violet bunches of fruit. The petunias take over the paths; a white cat lies in wait of its prey on the lawn. In spring time the roses appear, the dahlias in summer, in autumn chrysanthemums in such numbers as to touch your very heart. I have vague and mixed-up images that are reflected on the window panes above my mother's shoulders. They only last a very short time, like good feelings in your heart. They often originate in the plum trees, or the rhododendrons in accordance with the passing of the seasons; the sun might be shining or else it is raining, the tiny drops fall from the leaves like the seconds that tick by, gone for ever; and suddenly it's winter. The light branches of the Judas tree that have shed all their leaves form a type of stained-glass window with the blue sky shining through them. I'll have to hold on to all these images when mother has gone. There is but one Sunday now and it's always the last one. Mother's left hand half waves at me from behind the window, pulling back the curtain with her right hand at the very moment I've turned

66

the car around to head back to the city; yes, it's always the last time. I never thought of looking at her face during these departures; when you look at someone you're already separating yourself from them in some way.

> *Devance tout adieu*
> *Comme si cet adieu était derrière toi,*
> *Tel l'hiver qui s'achève.*
> *Car parmi les hivers est un hiver si long*
> *Qu'en hivernant, si tu survis, ton cœur vaincra.* *

Only one Sunday, one meeting. I had very little time, what with teaching, organising various events, giving talks. It was getting to the stage where I felt that I no longer had the words to express what I was feeling. I'd evade the questions people asked or else reply to them in an oblique manner. Being cultivated can isolate you, I said to myself in a pretentious manner. When you follow the cultural path you separate yourself from your own kind when they happen not to be intellectual. When I began writing, however, I felt that I was on the same level as my mother. Now I talk to her without trying to put myself on her wave-length, realising that the tone can be enough to convey meaning, the rhythm of the sentence. Or else the look I have when I'm talking can express a multitude. I always knew she was capable of seeing something beyond the mere words. We think we understand because we have reduced the vague world of impressions to the logic of comprehension. We have a thought to express each impression, a word. But anyone who doesn't know how to give a name to something has the possibility of reaching a far deeper level. Because when you name something you often don't know it or possess it except in an illusory manner. Thus it is that the poor who are fast asleep in what is beyond expression communicate better than we do with the

---

* Anticipate every goodbye, / as if this goodbye were already behind you, / just like the winter that is coming to an end. / Because among the winters is one winter so long, / that by getting throught it, / if you can survive, / your heart will win out.

67

invisible and the totality and, even if they happen to give in too easily to what is obscure, like magic or superstition, how can we know anymore the number of false revelations we ourselves submit to? After all, we constantly confuse the sign with the signified and we are often the proud prisoners of a universe of words that is fragmented and sterile.

I believe that I came to understand my relationship with the Church through my relationship with my mother. I wasn't very keen to introduce her to others, nor for her to be seen. The truth that she had within her was so secret and poor that it could only be betrayed by being publicly paraded in front of others. I was always fearful that, like a lady living in a posh area who comes out dressed in all her finery, wearing high heels, and gets lost in the poorer areas of the city, weighed down with her presents, people would point and laugh. I liked to meet my mother on my own or else with people of her acquaintance, who fed off her, who existed only through her but who never talked about this in a proud fashion.

Vis-à-vis many people in the Church I adopt a similar stance as with my mother: we don't always have the same language but we can understand and accept each other.

It was also thanks to my mother that I knew that it wasn't just a pharisaic attitude, as is often believed to be the case, that became attached to formulae and conventions, but also the deeply-felt faith that could spontaneously traverse the most ordinary images in order to commune with the living and true God. You shouldn't necessarily attack the formulae and conventions first of all, but the mediocrity of your soul.

My mother's language is simple, somewhat hackneyed, but maybe it's the very simplicity of it that allows it to convey itself. The richer and more clever language is, the more it tends to give way to self-satisfaction and prejudice. Of course, the prejudice is cleverly masked, according to the fashion of the day, which is what takes us in.

My mother's thoughts are conditioned; mine, probably a little less so. This is not as important as the ability to find in yourself, beyond all the conditioning, a movement that brings you a little further down the path of self-knowledge, as Malebranche would say. If you have to struggle against words, habit, the proliferation of religion at the expense of the Christian faith, it is not so much in order to purify the faith of the humble and the faithful, but to ensure that, in the eyes of those who are luke-warm about their religious practice, the outsiders, the ninety-nine lost sheep, faith ceases to appear insignificant and it takes root once more in their lives and hopes.

This could mean that there is no difference, for example, between Tieilhard de Chardin's God and the God of my mother. The images my mother uses – and on this issue I seek the indulgence of the enlightened, the doctors and the society ladies of the world – are no more an obstacle to my finding God than the images of my friend Teilhard. It appears that Teilhard is 'bringing back' a number of intellectuals to the Church. This is funny; I wonder if it's not just the latest device that the intellectuals have devised in order not to have to live faith in its exposed and demanding form. After all, on the intellectual level at least, Teilhard simply replaces one dialectic with another, one rationale with another, however paradoxical such words might appear in the context of faith. In the future, the mental construction of Teilhard, for which he is largely not responsible, will also seem dated, more dated even than that of Thomas Aquinas. We might reasonably want the intellectuals to listen more to the Bible, Paul of Tarsus, Meister Eckhart, John of the Cross, that they be less caught up in religion itself than in what constitutes a real Christian life. One could be fearful once more that they are beginning to adore the splendour of an intellectual image.

Mother was very sorry to see Latin dropped from Church services. She had learnt it off over the years in her bilingual Missal. It's awful now that everything can be understood so easily. One Sunday she said to me, 'What's this story about Beelzebub who comes back with seven spirits even more powerful than himself?' She asks such questions even though she knows instinctively that it's not really a question of seeing or understanding every single word; it has more to do with holding on to the essential message behind all this. She never questions the luke-warm and inflamed rhetoric of the priests in the church. Her purpose in listening to a sermon is not to determine whether it is good or bad – this is what most practising Catholics do – but to hold on to a sentence, or a word, which will provide enough food for her spiritual needs. The more often she goes to Church, the less she speaks about God, Christian duty, morality.

I believe that mother always lived beyond appearances. Anxious, indeed terrified when it came to her family, in case she might be falling down on her duty in some way like everybody else, all she had to keep her going at certain times was her simple religion, slightly superstitious, but which managed nonetheless to reassure her. There was something deep within her, perhaps it was her humble way of looking at life, or maybe it was the vague wave of pain that took hold of her when she heard someone talking about evil, but whatever it was, it proved indisputably that she had made a fundamental choice about her religion, or rather that that choice had been made within her. If she had had to choose for herself or for her family between the death of the body and the death of the soul, she would have gone for the former as Blanche de Castille did – she who had once appeared pretentious and ridiculous to me. For mother, we only have a certain length of time on this earth and we pass away in much the same way as day follows night and spring comes after winter. This spontaneous decision on her part to side with the Infinite against all the apparent seductions attendant on the immediate, against all the terrors, what Fichte refers to as the nostalgia for the eternal, always seemed to me to be the pre-requisite for faith, if it wasn't indeed faith itself. A person who retains a thirst for the eternal is already very close to the truth. I know those who chase after heaven on earth; I have walked alongside them in their quest. They grasp on to the first object that comes their way, saying, 'Am I happy now?' There is no point in their being sceptical, lucid; they seek out pleasures for themselves in a secretive manner along the way, earthly desires with which to replace divine hope. When the torrent of life finally ebbs from their body, however, they hear the voice from the bottom of their heart that says 'No'. Now they have to set about chasing the precious pearl once more, a love that will never fade, or else, if they have already stopped believing in such things, they'll seek out a thousand objects that might satisfy them for just a very brief moment. These plans, work, ambitions, fears, all the false illusions that are used to hide the void, are but a thousand heartbeats, a thousand flaps of the wings to achieve a more solid footing. We are in a big hurry to advance; all we're doing is running away. We achieve some height, but in reality we're falling down. Anything that will hide the vacuum that is at the heart of our existence is good. We buy things, sell them, get enmeshed in plots, push each other to succeed, get a promotion, think of the thrones and dominations that lie in front of us. From these dizzy heights, now that the ardour of youth has been left far behind us, we discover that the same malaise that we sought to escape from has not left us. 'Oh yes,' we say, 'wisdom consists of abandoning hope, because all that lies ahead is nothingness. I suppose we were lucky to have at least gotten something out of our lives.' Or, if people are believers, they beat their breasts, and tell us about the aspirations of their holy souls. And when the time comes for them to consider the reality of their own death, they are frightened because they wonder how they can be forgiven for having held on to their château, for remaining attached to worldly honours. All they can mutter over and over again is, 'Eternal life, eternal life'.

I think that the Christian can find some happiness in this life if he pays the price, just as my mother, it seems to me, sustained a profound peace through her little fears. Her words were simple, her thoughts naive. Nevertheless, it should be noted that it is not possible to trap God through intellectual discourse. We are floating in the eternal and in peace. All we have to do to ensure our happiness is to build fewer obstacles for ourselves and not to play on both sides of the fence. I, who have so often reacted belligerently to her ideas, her little devotional practices, would like to tell her this minute that she was wiser than the intellectuals who, after trying out all the good things in life, would like to have us believe that we should be happy with a little or wait till we're dead to find happiness. I'd like to say to her that she was more knowledgeable than the philosophers who nowadays are held in such high regard and who teach and proclaim everywhere they go that salvation can be found in the absence of salvation.

Mother was a great believer in blood relatives. She had a real flair for being able to name uncles and cousins, their children, their grandchildren, and it didn't make any difference whether they were living in the surrounding countryside, in the neighbouring cities or in Paris, she knew them from all over. She would have liked me to be better at remembering birthdays, visiting my relatives, attending all the baptisms, the marriages, the burials. There wasn't enough time in the year for all she'd like me to do. Anyway, I am not a great believer in birthdays. 'It's somebody's birthday every day, mother, I could be at parties all the time.' I was busy doing other things. In a sense, I was following my own predilection. I attempted to explain to her how it was, but, because I am not brave, I didn't tell her the full story. I had seen too many apostles, prophets, who reflected perfectly the prejudices of the village they were born into. They were happy to be their family's agents, notables and ambassadors of their own tribe who supported their nieces and nephews, and helped their clan to get on in life. It would be great to have national seminaries, I used to say to her. In that way you could place Parisians in Landernau or Perpignan, the Bretons in Grenoble or Marseille so they could benefit from the mountain air, the priests from the South of France could be placed in the North so they could acquire a more serious way of looking at life. In fact, I think it wouldn't matter at all where they were sent, while awaiting the inauguration of the Common Market of priests: it could be Germany, Italy, America, Africa, anywhere so long as they got to break the ancestral bonds, do away with local prejudices. When we are born, we inherit a family and a national order. The Cross proposes a new geometric location to us because it announces a truth that knows no borders, and bonds that have nothing to do with those of the flesh. It disintegrates society in order to reorganise it in a new way. It is strange that the link with the Cross was able to become in our minds, almost naturally, the social, family and national bond that cements everything together.

I didn't even attempt any more to express myself in a way that my mother would understand. I spoke freely or, in short, I gave vent to my anger. I believed that she was grateful to me for that much. She put forward objections, baulked at some of my statements. Every Sunday

I struggled against her, with her, just as I struggled against the Church, with it, for it. There was always some local event going on that led to disagreement, provoked an argument. A lot of this was because she watched television, read the main local newspaper, which glorified what was strong, humiliated what was weak. Such a newspaper only exists because of the appearances it cultivates. One Sunday there was the Sea Festival, for example. The Cardinal, surrounded by the priests, the local politicians, the army personnel, the whole gamut of local dignitaries, came to bless the sea. The boats, covered in bunting and flowers, floated happily in the water. Some hymns were sung to the sound of the bag-pipes. The cross was clearly visible in the midst of all this pomp. 'Isn't it just marvellous!', mother said. I said that I thought it was a scandal. 'Why do you have to use such words?' she asked. 'Mother, the only scandal as far as I am concerned is when the truth isn't announced.' I would have liked to add that the 'Blessing of the Sea' was organised by the rich ship-owners. The sailors were poorly paid, some earned a pittance and worked on boats in the most incredibly dangerous conditions. Any of them who happened to be Christians would have nothing to do with this sham of a celebration, which made religion an accomplice. Christianity was now no more than a part of the show.

She gave in easily enough on topics such as this one; she wasn't crazy about worldly celebrations in any case. She was more likely to resist me when it had to do with religious ceremonies. For example, one Sunday she was talking to me about the consecration of a new bishop, who was chosen in the diocese and was sent somewhere, I'm not sure exactly where. She was thrilled. She was amazed at how distant I appeared. The new bishop was a very nice, unassuming man. I knew him, in fact, and was rather delighted at his appointment. But the dreaded ceremony again made my blood boil – ten or twenty bishops were in attendance, protonotaries and prelates came from all parts of the world. There was a procession, unending ceremonies, men dressed up as if for the theatre came and went on the stage; I saw violet, purple, lots of croziers, mitres, glitz of all sorts, lights that flashed on and off, the solemn tones emanating from the organs. And then of course there was the lunch to follow, which was unending: up to five- or seven-hundred places set, seven speeches in which there was much talk of the Holy Spirit, of the second Vatican Council, charity, the greatness of France. There were thousands of bows made to the local dignitaries, the Prefect and the vice-Prefects. It wouldn't have mattered what religion these dignitaries were; they could have been Jews or Freemasons, notorious atheists, all that was of no consequence! Friends of mine who felt that they really had to attend reported back to me later that they were disgusted by the whole affair. Yes indeed, what difference did it make? Pontius Pilate or Caiphas should have been invited on Pentecost Sunday to show clearly that everybody was basically at one on the issue of the Resurrection. I exaggerated things slightly to get her to laugh; I ranted on a bit to give the impression that I wasn't taking myself too seriously. The word scandal came back a few times.

'Do you really think that one can think what you have . . . ?'

'Of course,' I said, 'in another fifty years people will have as much difficulty believing that this sort of practice went on as . . . '

It wasn't difficult for me to understand the sort of people who attended these ceremonies. After all, many were there out of friendship, or out of a spirit of faith. And then again there were many others who were full of the ideas of Vatican II. This was their family get-together. But my God, why couldn't they listen for a while to the conversations of the non-believers or to the Christians who weren't out of the ordinary but who at least were concerned at being logical in their disbelief. When would they know themselves intimately, when would they feel deep down that all these overly spectacular celebrations are, in a very precise way, nothing less than a scandal? Not only because at the same time as these ceremonies are going on there are signs up on the doors of churches, and notices everywhere, saying that millions of people are going to die of hunger, but more so because the only scandal that matters is that the truth is hidden under such lavish appearances.

Was I just reacting out of pride, or pomposity even? When do you have the right to stand up against something? 'Whatever I think won't change anything,' I said to her. 'And I don't want everything to change immediately. What would become of me if everything was perfect? I'd be unemployed and I'd have nothing to gripe about. But everyone should say whatever he has to say while waiting for the revelation to take place. This will happen when the time is ripe.'

If she wouldn't let go, I had one weapon I held in reserve. I went and got the Bible. 'It's not only the baddies who protest,' I said to her. 'Listen to what Amos has to say about the true religion:

> "*I hate, despise your ceremonies*
> *For your solemn services I have but disgust*
> *Your offerings, I throw back at you*
> *Lead me far away from your songs,*
> *Let me hear no more the sound of your harps*
> *And let Justice flow upon you*
> *Like a torrent that never dries up.*"'

I thought I was on top, my triumph seemed assured. But suddenly she struck a blow at the Achilles' heel.

'Are you certain that you're not searching for your own comfort in all this? You yourself want a religion that suits you.'

I was trapped. It took me a long time to regain my composure.

'Yes, of course I'm looking for happiness like everyone else. However, what I feel is shared by many others. Many have abandoned a religion that seemed to them to be removed from life. What I'm looking for, no, what I've found, is a faith that inspires my life and that is beginning to concern all those who go their different ways about finding God. Yes, you have a point, I am looking for my own happiness. But religion makes you happy as well. We feel the same way, and yet we have different ways of dealing with the problems that religion poses. God will recognise His own.'

And, saying this, I burst out laughing.

Mother, whose loyalty to her religion was unwavering, who was not content simply to follow the commandments but also sought spiritual advice on certain issues she was unsure of, almost never talked about duty or principles. The more she prayed the more she came to love life; this fact never ceased to amaze me. Just a few years ago now she happened to be complaining, like everybody else, about the depravity of young people. Nonetheless, she was now no longer annoyed by the variety shows on the television that catered mainly for these same young people – in fact, she found them quite amusing.

'Yes, of course, mother, good Christians sing their hymns of joy in the churches. But wouldn't you admit that they don't often look too happy? These light-hearted, immature young people hardly ever have a thought for God; rather, they're singing a hymn of joy to life, which they appear to believe in. What they don't seem to realise is that God is also on the side of life.'

I amazed her with such pronouncements, but she accepted me as I was. However, she couldn't resist trying to bring me back into the world in which she lived. I should have just given in, let her have her little moment of happiness. I am aware of this unyielding side to my character, this intransigence which is very strong in me and which I dislike. At this stage in my life I should be well and truly cured of my past but it's obvious that I'm not.

'You only come on flying visits; nobody knows you around here. Other priests who have their family in the area come and give sermons – I see them at the ceremonies. And I'm told that you give such good sermons.'

I knew the point she was making but I was absolutely terrified by narrow customs such as these – the daily life of the village where everybody knows everybody else, the rituals – this rhythm of life had become alien to me. How can you go back in time, force yourself to believe what you no longer believe, say what others want to hear? I had found my solution in my weekly little drive on Sundays. I'd arrive just as the bells were announcing the beginning of high Mass. It would have been too difficult to explain to her how these ceremonies exasperated me, the sermons, everything about them. How could I convey to her that I didn't want to walk again over the paths of my childhood? I wasn't even able to tell her that she herself was the only link I had to the village, to rural civilisation; that sort of talk would only have confused her more. I no longer had the necessary language to communicate with her world. I didn't want to shock or cause a scandal to anyone and yet I couldn't lie either by trying to root out words from my past. I wasn't trying to give the impression that I didn't appreciate the work done by priests in the parishes. I admired their devotion, their clear-headedness about their work. They were poor, they had to endure solitude all their active lives and witness the desertion of organised religion by their flock without becoming too discouraged. There are even some priests now who are preparing, in secret, pockets of Christians who will light up the world of the future. But their attitude is often foreign to me; it's as if they're speaking Chinese. Schools, elections, donations to the Church, drama groups, music, repairing the bell tower, buying a new organ, I couldn't endure this. They have been placed there to work with what little there is, to keep the show on the road. They accomplish their mission, so how could anyone hold it against them?

One day I brought home a naked cross that a sculptor friend of mine had given me, done in the modern style. It wasn't difficult to see that she wasn't very enthusiastic about this gift.

'Oh, it's much too lovely for me. What will people think?'

But the doubts she was really harbouring finally surfaced.

'What has your artist friend done with Our Lord?'

'He could no longer find him on the cross,' I replied. 'Have you forgotten that the nails were removed from his hands and feet, that he was taken down from the cross, buried, rose again? The cross is empty. We should really be talking about the one who was decrucified. The cross is empty, which means that there are millions of people who now replace Christ on it every day, whether by choice or by necessity. Christ alone has escaped ahead of everyone else until He comes back among us on the Last Day.'

She gave a shrug of incomprehension. A few months went by and then one Sunday morning she said to me, 'It's funny but I'm getting used to your cross with, what did you call him, yes, the Decrucified one. On seeing it, I now think less about Our Lord and more about all those people who have to endure pain and I pray for them. Do you think this is a better way for me to act, Mr Know-it-all?'

Now that my books were beginning to be published, mother no longer said to me, 'You're always writing, scribbling things down'. Instead she asked me, 'Why do you write?' I could see that her question was born of anxiety, as if she had a foreboding about all that was considered impure about literature. Her question, it seemed to me, wanted to inquire, 'Are you writing so that people will talk about you, or to earn money?' But I saw something else deep down in the look she focused on me: 'Is this just a roundabout way for you to give up on your vocation?' I varied my responses from day to day. She forced me to see myself as I was. Here are a few examples of the answers I gave her:

'I write because I am not fit to do anything else, mother.'

Or:

'I write to get a good mark. I'm still like a schoolboy handing in his homework.'

Or:

'I write in order to be read by friends, to meet others through my writing.'

One Sunday I said to her:

'I write because of you, mother.'

Mother loved telling stories. For a long time I hadn't paid any attention to her stories, but I was beginning to find in my memory very clear images that had been carefully sculpted by her. Like the time she told me about how, as a little girl, a fire had started not far from her parents' farm. I could hear the alarm bell going off, imagine the terrified little girl with her face glued to the window. Seventy years later I could see all this, I could look into the eyes of the horse who was going wild with fright and whose mane was flowing in the wind and whose hooves were making the ground shudder, the half-naked man who mounted it and shouted, 'Fire! Fire!' I had no difficulty making out the little girl running frantically across the fields, the human chain formed by men and women who, in the light of the flames, passed buckets of water to one another while laughing, boys and girls leaving the human chain for no reason, running after each other, throwing each other on the grass, their high-pitched squeals of laughter, and mother being so horrified that people could play in this way when there was such misfortune in front of their eyes. In fact, it turned out to be nothing at all, just a haystack that had caught fire. 'I like to tell stories in the way that you tell them,' I said to her.

Naturally, I would have loved to explain to her that I wrote in order to find myself, to find God who is already found, never found, to discover a hidden path. That sort of explanation would have been too extreme, and yet I believe genuinely that that is the reason why I began writing. I had no interest any more in knowing what constituted literature. Indeed, I didn't feel compelled to worry at all about literature. Writing, it seemed to me, limited my chances of telling lies. I felt I had to write against myself, against those who were close to me. In brief, I needed to struggle against prejudice through my writing. Maybe it would have suited my purposes if I had been able to find clear signs of my having been specially chosen to write in my childhood. I didn't manage to find any, however. Obviously, I was never going to be a great writer. I'd hand in my homework on time, be a diligent worker, dig down deep enough in my inner being in order to reach that which is shared by all underneath our differences. I'd express myself and by extension the faith that was peculiar to me while hoping not to betray anything: such was my manifest ambition. It is true, however, that clear thinking can also hide all sorts of obscure cravings. How should we set about escaping the vile abomination engendered by advertising, which was always giving judgements, exalting one writer, humiliating another, making this person into a celebrity, that person into a nobody according to criteria that, rather frequently, had nothing whatever to do with language. Why should I drag my mother into this absurd universe of vanity, pretentiousness and exaggeration? So I settled for the explanation that seemed to me to be the deepest, or in any case, the best: 'I write in order to be read by friends, to meet new friends.'

It is difficult to speak without a mask, especially if you wish to reach the literary specialists, who have often ruined their souls by reading too many things and, yet, without whom you never get any readers. You have to cheat, that is to say, transform your most inner truth into a literary truth. You are ruined if you don't succeed in separating the man from the artist. Readers more often than not are used to this, to the literary games that are played between the writer and his public. People are afraid of anything that might burn them. But if you succeed in hiding your message beneath all the literary devices possible, everybody declares unanimously: 'What truth you find in this writing! What authenticity!'

They believe they know what a writer who is also a priest can or cannot say. They have constructed stereotyped images of the clergy since their childhood, through all the prejudices they have been exposed to, be they pious or not, through the habits they have formed, the scruples. They stand there in judgement and express their outrage in an enthusiastic manner. Some, who took part in bygone struggles and who believe themselves still to be very much in the know, have improved their image, they believe they have very liberal ideas on things. Such blindness removes any obligation they might feel to judge fairly. But it is still a stereotype they are putting forward. I consider these people the worst when it comes to assessing my work. Seated in their comfortable armchairs, they make value judgements about what is good and bad about morality, theology, without anyone ever being able to find out how they became qualified to pronounce on such matters. In truth, they have scarcely advanced beyond the basic catechism of perseverance. Still, they have all the advantages, they hold the trump cards.

'Excuse me, Father . . .' They really impede your discourse when they say 'Father.' Since *The Provincial Letters* [Pascal], addressing someone in this way has all sorts of undertones over which you have no control. 'Father, do you mind telling us how you can hold in your consecrated hand the . . . and still have the nerve to write such things?' You'd like the ground to open up and swallow you. They have not moved on from the traditional image of the priest, the minister of all that is sacred, a Magus, magician, puppet, teacher. They are incapable of understanding that a priest is alive, that he has a human heart, a voice that should seek to change life itself, announce the other world that is present even in our earthly existence, in art, love, anything you like. They would be amazed, shocked, were you to put forward the idea of a man who happens to be a writer and also a priest, and who has no wish to comment, give sermons, adjure, convince but rather to baptise the world, live it in the fullness of its reality. They cannot imagine how such a person, through his particular temperament and character, without losing his head, can rediscover the true vocation of the world with all that is good and bad within it. No, they just like to see the priest in his vestments, leading a procession or officiating at a ceremony; they'd like to tell him to go back to saying his *oremus*.

To my way of looking at things, they are just like the rich man of the Gospel, at least a few of them are! And then, of course, there are those who say, 'We're here, we'll follow you.' These would be situated at the head of the procession, they'd take part in all the various conferences organised by the Church. In other words, they'd follow you but they'd give up nothing. They may well tell you their stance with regard to the Blessed Trinity, their idealistic aspirations, even the sadness they have endured in their lives. Yet when push comes to shove, they will not agree to give up anything. Bedecked in gold, blessed among men, highly regarded because of their insights, the calm assurances they give for want of ideas, they are the Great Defenders of Religion, of Morality, false martyrs who would like to have us believe that their faith is rocked by every blow they receive. They are mere mirrors, reflections of others' thoughts, overly loyal subjects of a Christendom that may well have sincerely decided on a return to humility and poverty, but that continues, for the present, to be the prisoner of former reflexes and, through a chasm that has developed between its intentions and its actions, has come to rely on power and prestige as heavily as in the past. Here they are pouring scorn on a film one minute, a book the next, rushing to the rescue of orthodoxy. They come across as being more traditionally Catholic than any ten bishops you could find, beautifully unaware that they are the spokesmen for a specific milieu, a clientele of sorts. When have they studied up on these issues? Where? Did they get up in the morning and suddenly have an in-depth knowledge of a living theology that uplifted their souls? What are they doing wasting their time railing against what they call the literature of decomposition? Whatever is degrading and evil should be left alone. Both those who exploit the ambivalence with regard to vice and trivialise it, as well as those who sit in judgement on them, should equally be left to their own devices. There have been groups, censorship boards set up for that type of thing. Pontiffs, whether Christian or not, happy in their role and in their culture, sicken me. I am not shocked in any way by the literature of decomposition: it is a normal manifestation in a society such as the one we live in, just as paganism is natural. At least it breaks through the veneer of self-satisfaction and reveals the void at the heart of existence. We expect great men to give us a larger vision of life and not to simply pander to public opinion like the scribes and the pharisees. Life is capable of protecting itself perfectly well.

The writers I referred to earlier appear to me as if they want to represent the views of society, of a certain order that has been established, to prolong mental habits; in brief, they're nothing but bigots. What outsider, what unbeliever, would have the nerve to formulate the theory of the transcendence of faith, even in a careful, meandering and oblique language? All he would see in that sort of reasoning would be the manoeuvrings of the social climber. The language of prostration, which is also that of the spiritual desert, especially if it has a noble tone, does more to lift my heart than the literature of decomposition. The Knights of the Wisdom of Nations are farther removed from Christian madness than our profligate youth.

I'll say one very simple thing: I am frightened by the certainty of these so-called literary experts, by their self-assured arrogance. The appreciative sounds they make about talented writers, maybe even writers of genius, is disturbing. Think of the scene the writers could make if they wanted to, but instead they remain silent. Where are the prophets, I ask myself? In truth, literature has become a career for many writers. There is an obvious contradiction between pursuing a career and living out the paradoxes of the Gospel. I keep on waiting to hear a breath, a voice of rebellion. Instead, all we're treated to is writers playing around with political or moral ideas and telling us about their pious aspirations. All I hear are well-rounded, balanced truths that will not upset the apple cart.

In truth, I find in these writers the religion of my mother with its attachments to pious practices. But my mother, at least, had no chance to go beyond this simple approach. Her type of religion didn't at all prevent her from reaching the living and true God; what's more, she wasn't addressing any audience. I have never doubted for a moment that the successful Christian writers of our time – our own crop if you like – do not serve the true God, but, since they are addressing the world, why couldn't they at least have left behind them so many loyalties that no longer hold any credence? Could they not break through the barriers placed in their way by the devout people, invent not only a literary style, but a life style? Could they not stop being lords and pay the price demanded by Christ from his followers?

I can't stand it any more; I'm jealous. I am pained when I see certain writers who are only interested in money, who are accused of being such or who admit it themselves. You have no difficulty reading what they write, they are not tetchy or hard to approach and how sad I am to see them deliberately standing back from things, fleeing the stupid honours that are available when at the same time some of our own are allowing themselves be showered with praise, blessed by the literary establishment. And to think that they call themselves witnesses! It's obvious that they are serving the cause of literature, it's possible that they're serving religion, but they are definitely not serving the cause of faith in its highest truth. You can't be so well in with the powers that be, the great leaders, those who say they represent the highest values, while at the same time being moved at the sight of the son of man being crucified! Is it not revealing to think that young people have only been following the atheistic thinkers for a long time. What they demand is some coherent logic. Don't believe for a second that they are going to listen to potentates; they're much too independent-minded for that.

I sometimes shared thoughts of this type with my mother. It was stupid, pretentious, I know. She hadn't a clue what I was on about; I was just letting off steam. With her, I could let myself go, nobody was really listening. I seemed to be playing at being the prophet, but really I was just being myself. Was it the fault of the powerful Catholics that Bernanos died? Was it their fault that they didn't know how to look after the flock? Brought up as part of a privileged tribe, they only knew what it was to live in a privileged world. I didn't really want to pass judgement on them. I would be worse myself in the same situation. It might have just been envy that was gnawing away at my insides. But in the end I wasn't trying to be fair-minded. Rightly or wrongly there was a feeling I shared with many others and of that I was sure: the immense deception at having seen so many writers – Catholics like myself – and to still see so many of them, categorised, easily explained, who have no significance whatsoever outside of the literary context. One day, at the risk of being pulverised, I would have to say what was burning inside me. I might be ashamed to speak out but I'd be even more ashamed to stay quiet. One day I would take the microphone, since nobody else was raising his voice, since everybody seemed to find what was happening natural. Maybe I would just speak so that the rebels, who were going to be the Christians of the future, might know that all Christians didn't feel solidarity with their ecclesiastical leaders, no more than with Chateaubriand, Henri Bordeaux or those who followed them.

Unfortunately, I wasn't up to the task I set myself. A peasant when it came to culture, that's the only way you could describe me. Everything came out in too aggressive a manner. I had no desire to paint pretty pictures, to add polish to what I was saying so that people would remark, 'This guy has some serious talent. Jesus, do you see the way he writes!' The world is full of books, books with buckets of talent displayed in them, well-constructed phrases that could be sweet or sharp as a razor blade, admirable. In such works dazzling things are offered to you, mirrors in which the fundamental anguish and boredom of the aesthetes are reflected. I preferred books that had a bit of everything, that were difficult to grasp and that permitted you to lose yourself in order to find a new you. In them I could hear the untamed interior voice that cries out in every human being, a heartbeat, a sign of life. You are not meant to admire these books but to start afresh because of them.

Mother read any reviews of my books that she could find in the newspapers. It was all double-Dutch to her but she liked to see my name mentioned and to find out if they were saying nice things about me. For a long time the religious newspapers never said a word about my books. She didn't know what to make of this. It needed a strong person to take the lead in these publications. The silence bothered my mother a lot, she thought the worst.

On the odd occasion I'd bring some illustrious figure to see her on a Sunday. I know two or three of this sort who, although they have climbed far up the ladder of social success, can still remember who their friends are. I would say to myself, 'This will reassure her a lot more than anything I say.' But, on meeting these people, she became so obsequious, so frightened of saying something wrong, or of speaking incorrectly, that I concluded that it was merely an ordeal for her. It was almost as if she was listening to herself speak. If only she could have let herself go! She must have been frightened of me, she must have actually believed that I was keeping a watchful eye over all her words and actions.

Another Sunday I found her on the verge of tears. The previous week, a soft-spoken priest, on his own initiative, had come to tell my mother – and for my own good, mind you! – that I was heading down a slippery slope, that she shouldn't be afraid, of course; she could, after all, suggest that I . . . In any case, he was aware of how attached I was to my mother . . . In brief, he was engaging in emotional blackmail. This man was considered to be a 'saint', but piety can go hand in hand with blindness and the virtuous person doesn't always see things as they are. I had to get an influential priest friend to explain to my mother that censorship wasn't like a sacrament that priests could hand out as they saw fit. After all, a cardinal had given me his vote of confidence. As for myself, I rooted out letters that a bishop had sent me and I read them to her. Long before he knew who I really was, this man would write to me every time one of my books was published. He continued this trend after discovering my true identity. 'Don't worry unduly about the knocks you will get,' he wrote. 'Don't despise yourself if you don't feel equal to the high standards you propose in your writing. Endure all this and make sure that you don't compromise in what you are saying. Remember, your voice is not just your own, but also that of many of your readers.' I am happy that this bishop will know from these lines that he gave a little heart to an old woman who didn't know much about literature.

It was for her, and for her peace of mind, that I agreed to come out of the shade a bit. When I was twenty-five, Daniel-Rops had been a friend of mine to whom I owed a lot. At that point, he had been a very well-known public figure. Then he had given up writing novels and had begun writing in a new, more marketable manner and had ended up with a chair in the Académie Française. For a long time I had been of the opinion that we had moved apart, that we had nothing in common any more. Then, out of the blue, Daniel-Rops, having read my novel, *Mais il y a la mer* [The Sea Remains], wrote to me to say that it had a good chance of winning the Catholic Prize for Literature that year. I had done what he had believed impossible – to write and still remain detached from the world. Still, every writer, and I was no exception, needs readers. When I began writing I didn't know that the literary world was composed of little cliques and idols; I was perfectly content to be ignorant of this fact in the beginning. I very quickly came to realise, however, the difficulty my marginal position posed if I wanted to enlarge my readership. The Catholic press totally ignored me, the non-Catholic press paid scarcely any attention to books that dealt with themes that were obviously Christian. In the beginning I had wanted to exist in a literary context in which language would be the primary consideration, along with tone of course. I was being very naive, maybe even a little proud. The Catholic Prize for Literature would place me in too narrow a literary category. This is the reason why I hesitated for such a long time about accepting it. Daniel-Rops wrote to tell me that I'd have to make up my mind one way or the other. He seemed so sure that it was the right thing for me to do! It was the thought of my mother that finally won the day. I said to myself, 'She will read so many positive things about my writing in *La Croix* that she'll have no more worries about me.'

So I got my invitation announcing that I was the winner of the Catholic Prize for Literature, which guaranteed that I would have more readers. But at what a price! Of course, a controversy then arose, which I'm ashamed to talk about because it was so trivial. People had looked for, and found, documents that said I had unconventional ideas, that it would be difficult to be sure of my good character. I was informed of what was happening. Somebody had broken the bond of secrecy – a rotten thing to do. So, all of a sudden there I was, obliged to defend myself, to produce sworn evidence to the fact that I was a bona fide Catholic. Now I needed to give the impression that I desperately wanted what I had only accepted initially with reluctance. In truth, I had unknowingly placed myself in an awful situation. Daniel-Rops moved quickly to squash any remaining doubts that people may have been harbouring about me and he achieved what amounted to a false diplomatic unanimity. It was as good as in the bag.

Finally the big day arrived, and the writer headed off to the prize-giving ceremony. He hung around in the fourteenth arrondissement to pass a bit of time before everything was scheduled to begin. On arrival at the building in which the ceremony was to take place, as the door was opened for him, he noticed that it led down to a huge corridor covered in a rich, red carpet. At the end of the corridor he had the time to see a conference room, lit up, full of cameras, women's dresses, jewellery, priests, the violet colour of some Monsignors' garb. Then he saw some men who were seated in a line on either side of the corridor, right beside the door. They appeared to be the members of the jury. Not one of them acknowledged his presence apart from Daniel-Rops. The prize-winner went forward, extended his hand. There was consternation written on all the faces; their eyes turned away rapidly. Eventually Daniel-Rops took his arm and dragged him into an office where he was to be hidden from view. He had arrived five minutes early. The jury must first of all meet to make official a decision already known for the past fortnight – that's the ritual in these things. The minutes passed. He felt a sudden strong impulse to flee. What joy it would have given him if he could tell them to go and stuff their ceremony. But then he thought about his mother who would read *La Croix* the following morning. After ten minutes he saw the mask-wearing judges from the corridor rushing towards him, suddenly very warm, waxing lyrical about his book. 'Congratulations! You've produced an admirable novel.' And with that, he was dragged underneath the lights. The cameras now shot into action; he was surrounded by journalists, they put a copy of the book in his hand that he must place like this over his chest. 'Could you turn this way, please? Thank you.' He felt like he was making his First Communion all over again, overcome as he was by all this attention. And this man was supposed to be a rebel! During the pouring of champagne, the well-heeled ladies made appreciative noises about what he had written, this group of people who all knew each other, met again, congratulated each other, he could hear the comment that should be addressed straight to him – it rumbled like a volcano within him: 'You're nothing but an impostor. You describe a cardinal who turns his back on his exalted position within the Church to follow a more humble path. He ends up a lowly criminal and is left to rot in jail. And you, the writer who brought this cardinal to life, you dare to show yourself thus in public, to lap up all this praise!'

Shortly afterwards, I realised that I had got myself all worked up for no good reason. The Prize was not a very significant one, just a painful moment I had to endure. In the end I wasn't as indifferent as I had thought I was to the vain pleasure you can feel at seeing your photo in the newspaper, or on the television. That at least gave me the impression that I existed, that I had a place in the literary world, because some serious-minded people would now find that my books were good. And then again, maybe my sadness was just the result of this – once more it hadn't anything to do with me, they were building up a certain image of the writer to suit the particular set of circumstances. But even this made me more proud than before. At the same time, I think there was a part of me that was happy that my success was modest, given that it had been obtained because the jury misunderstood my message. Knowing exactly how the game had been played, I couldn't fail to remember that choosing me was simply down to chance and the influence of a person with whom I was friendly.

That evening there was a dinner in the sixteenth arrondissement. Not one of the Catholic writers I knew and admired was there. I quickly understood the reason why: it was difficult to breathe in this type of atmosphere.

'For years now I haven't been going out in the evenings,' Daniel-Rops said to me. He was already showing many of the signs of a serious illness. 'However, I will make an exception to be with you tonight.'

What was he afraid of, I wonder. I suppose he realised that to a certain extent I had gatecrashed the party. There was a lack of human warmth at the dinner table. A writer, who had been detained at sea, had composed a scholarly address for the occasion which was now read out by somebody or other. He referred to the ancient Breton faith, the granite rocks and the savage ocean spray that could make life seem like a constant Calvary. He was really overstepping the mark. At a certain stage, Daniel-Rops leaned towards me and whispered: 'You have finally made it as a writer.' I replied, 'I fear those writers who become successful. They have often betrayed something essential.'

Daniel-Rops seemed exhausted. Tears were flowing from his sick eyes underneath his dark glasses. He obviously could sense the extent to which I felt like an outsider. I must have looked tense, maybe even on the point of exploding. He placed his hand on mine for a second and said, 'You will be read, that's what counts.' This was the last image I would have of him. I had always suspected that beneath his public image was hidden a secret and largely unknown entity.

'I'd like to thank you for the pleasure this will give my mother,' I said to him.

I walked for a long time in Paris that night. I made a vow to myself, or something unconsciously made the vow within me, not that I would be free exactly, that's a resolution without meaning, but that I would keep my distance from the literary establishment by adopting the means that would allow me to talk freely. I write this today in the hope that a friend will extend the hand of friendship to me if I ever happen to fall back into the trap of edification.

Mother was happy and started reading my books with some enthusiasm. They caused her untold problems. She had only ever read Pierre l'Ermite, the novels that form the *Veillée des Chaumières* series.

'Why do you have to mix everything up?' she asked me one day. 'You often start your books at the end, you jump from the past to the future; I have difficulty following what's going on.'

'Everyday time seems to be true, mother, nicely measured for us by clocks, but that is just an illusion. In fact, time is constantly disintegrating. Take us, for example – we were opposite each other at this table but we will never again be in that time framework. We move on.'

'But if, for example,' she said, 'next Sunday . . .'

'No, every day is the last, every second the last. When you dream, you constantly flit from the past to the present, to the future. Or even when you only remember something, it's not the dates that are important. Only what is essential comes back. When God considers our lives on earth, he might only retain two or three things. He sees everything in one glance. We have been taught to accept only what is logical, the time of the clock and the calendar, for example. It's practical when you want to catch a train, wish someone a happy birthday, but all that is false. Fundamentally, you never know what time it is. The writer is not just someone who writes stories, mother; rather, he is someone who has another truth that he is trying to convey. For me, a Christian, writing involves attempting to capture eternity underneath all that passes by in front of my eyes, a time of liberty, and of joy also.'

She was delighted with this interpretation; she found it reassuring. Still, she had difficulty understanding how you could write in a Christian fashion without mentioning God, the saints, or without imparting a moral lesson of some sort.

'It's reading Pierre l'Ermite that has put that into your head,' I said to her.

She thought that people read to relax, to pass the time and that it was the same with writing. How could she have been expected to think in any other way when writers and intellectuals have long held the same position on the issue?

One day I was frightened and surprised to find myself writing about my mother. What's worse is the fact that I was writing about her in the past tense. It's only with great vagueness that you see those whom you love and so you don't attempt to describe them. You exist with them, that's all. Writing supposes a sort of detachment – was I already saying goodbye to her from a faraway shore?

I have said how I liked to hide my mother from public view in former times. More recently, I had become proud of her, her long hair with not the slightest hint of grey. At seventy-five you'd think she was only sixty. In conversations with others, I'd often begin with, 'My mother . . .' When my mother was alive I didn't understand the secret hurt looks that came onto people's faces. Now, if anybody says 'My mother . .' I feel the sharp teeth of memory digging into my heart.

One of our trees, a cypress in fact, which seemed to be thriving, started dying suddenly for no apparent reason. I had it cut down and, to obliterate any possible reminder of it, I was quick to design a rose bed in its place. 'All you're missing now is a cross,' my mother said.

It did in fact look like a tomb, situated as it was under the large blue cypress trees, which in areas like ours grow strong when dead people are buried near them - cypress trees are commonly found in cemeteries. I quickly changed the location of my flower bed.

Superstitious fears were beginning to take hold of me. I engaged in some magic practices: I moved the stones on the pathway to the side, cleared away the special wire with which mother tied up the dahlias, carnations and gladioli that cluttered up the pathways. I was terrified she might fall and break her hip. 'Please,' I begged her. 'Don't go down to the cellar any more.'

I would still come across her, when I'd arrive unexpectedly, in the seed-loft, which was in the attic, watching the different matches and the fairs that were going on beyond the wall of our garden. She had such a great desire to see things, such a zest for life! 'Don't worry', she'd say, 'I'm holding onto the banister. You must take me for an old woman?'

She was as hardy as a young country girl. I'd worry about her in a hypocritical manner all week because of the few hours I spent with her on Sunday. I should, of course, have stayed near her, if I was that worried, let the time go by until she went to meet her Maker. I think I may have been afraid to become too attached to her.

Signs do not float completely outside of our bodies – our fears create them and then they become heightened as time goes by more quickly and they cannot find any object on which to rest. In this way the hypochondriac ends up being right about his imagined illnesses. And the optimist is found to be a fool when it comes to considering the final end, which is always tragic.

In the past the harmony that is to be found in all of Bach's music annoyed me in the same way as the church bells are said to annoy Satan. The cantatas, the suites, spoke of a peaceful kingdom of which I wanted no part. It was at that time I began listening to Bach. I had just come back from a trip to India. Bach's music had some of the transparent light that you find above the river Cavery, or over the Trimourti at Elephanta, and of the Shiva caught up in his circle of fire. It spoke of Vishnu in his struggle with the serpent representing Eternity; and of course it evoked Meister Eckhart. I felt no emotion at all this and yet the tears started flowing, bringing in their wake strange images; the faces of dead people, long forgotten, whose eyes were closed, living people who were already dead. It was as if time had stopped and an almost impersonal conscience was pushing me very far away. I saw my mother stretched on her bed, with her rosary beads in her hands, replying to the prayers of those who were in the throes of death. It was as if some angel had taken pity on me by trying to gently show me the suffering that lay ahead.

I was posing for a photograph when the blow struck, on the avenue Montaigne. A friend, who was was somehow employed in the experiments they were doing on the bomb out in the beautiful Pacific, had given me the key of his apartment for the two years he would be away. A review had sent a photographer to take some shots. 'But of course you have to oblige, it's absolutely vital that you do so. This magazine specialises in colour photographs, a process that is unique in Europe. No way you can get out of this one, Sulivan, I'm afraid.'

I was posing with very bad grace, but in the end I co-operated with everything: how could I do otherwise? If you write, you want to be read. By some miracle, an international magazine had been taken with what I wrote. Once more I said to myself, 'Maybe I am a writer after all!'

'Relax, be natural. It would be great to get a shot of you in the window. Hold on, from the balcony we can get the whole sweep of the avenue. Can you lean forward just a tiny bit? Great, that way we can fit in Sacré-Coeur in the background. I hadn't realised that you could see Montmartre from the avenue Montaigne. Come on, now, I told you to relax!'

The phone rang. I heard the timid voice of the secretary. 'There has just been a call from your family in Brittany. Your mother is tired, yes, very tired.' It was obvious that the secretary didn't want to worry me, hurt me by her words. 'Your brother said to tell you not to go home by car under any circumstances.' And all this time the guy with his cameras and projectors delayed his departure from the apartment for what seemed like an interminable period.

There was no question of going home by car then. A fog prevented me from seeing faces and things around me. I could only observe my upper lip trembling like the lips of a rabbit smelling cabbage. The taxi was going nowhere in the traffic, we were trapped in a long line of cars that were bumper to bumper. We were only moving ten metres every five minutes and we were enveloped in a cloud of carbon monoxide gas. There was no way out; where would we go in all this traffic? All the occupants of the cars looked unperturbed, no one was shouting. They had probably been tamed by many such experiences.

'Listen, I'll double your fare if you get me to the station in time for my train,' I said.

'You should have told me that before now,' he replied. 'We could have taken a detour. Hold on, in five minutes we'll get out of this mess. Trust me, I know how to make up time in this city.'

I recognised my panic, the desire to flee, to disappear. Enduring passion is the same for everyone, whatever the cause. We always experience awful dizziness when we realise that our mortal flesh is vulnerable, that it collapses finally under the strain of living. How quickly the years passed by! Forms and sounds became dim, the countryside was shifting uncontrollably. Love was like death; I had never known up to this point what it was like to fall into nothingness. Mother's face was erased, forgotten like you forget the wine that you drink, the hard times you go through. I didn't know yet that human desire can often assume the mask of pity, of softness and of disavowal. A friend of mine had once grabbed me by the hair to stop me from falling into the abyss towards which I was heading, thus saving me from the ignoble tragi-comedy of desperation in much the same way as you give a violent slap to someone who has been rescued from drowning. A friend, a silent well: we hadn't become friends in a real sense, however. It's just our eyes that don't forget when our glances meet. Someone like this is even more important than a friend.

When the time came for me to make a crucial decision, I had rushed to my mother, collapsed in her loving embrace. This was the only time I ever saw her not busy tidying stuff away. How had I found the courage to tell her these things? Had I really come so close to death? She had been so fearful-looking: she hadn't uttered a word one way or the other. What I could remember now, in this train that was bringing me to her, was the way her eyes focused on me, her silence. It had to be at that precise moment that our relationship had changed, that she no longer looked on me as a woman does on her son. She became more than a mother, something far more precious, a friend. Because she hadn't held me back in any way I was linked to her forever and, through her, to the Church of which she, as well as some other special friends I had, was one of the most palpable signs.

On two occasions I would subsequently be brought home bleeding and in a coma. My experiences with powerful motorbikes had the advantage at least of teaching me how to overcome certain fears. Crazy young people who feel it necessary to rev up their engines don't bother me; I feel at home among them. Their pointless passions will one day find an outlet and it is my prayer that this outlet be on a par with a boundless desire. Every time my mother's eyes were on me. She sometimes seemed aloof to me, enigmatic, as if she had already said goodbye. Again today it struck me that I was heading towards her to tell her about some unfortunate thing that had happened to me so that she could console me. I know it's stupid but that's the way I felt.

Obviously I didn't have any of these exact thoughts on the train; my heart was as hard as a stone. But now that I'm writing about what happened, images are flooding back that I thought I had never had.

Is there any real point in sharing this mediocre account with my readers? After all, why add to everybody's anxieties, everybody's wounds? I'm only increasing the pile of useless descriptions already in existence. Could you not at least try to produce something enlightening on this topic, Sulivan? You must make up your own minds on these matters, my friends, for I can never be a model for anyone. I write with whatever comes to hand. I would love to find again and to display in the Word the shiver that travels down people's spines when they are exposed to something more than the anecdotes that happen to everybody. Do you believe that my purpose in writing is to edify? I am looking for a truth that has been found and that is never found. I write to give thanks, perhaps with the idea that what is most intimate in our lives is also the most universal and, consequently, the most common. In order to feel less ashamed, it would obviously be sufficient to say my little parcel of truth in my own voice, a voice that is not just mine but that is at the heart of every human being.

Now I'll tell you about my mother's death.

When you go into a hospital it's like going through the doors of a world governed by its own laws, which stands apart from the usual human bonds. The patient was behind a glass screen: I was allowed to nod at her from a distance. Human sentiments only spread chaos in this new order. I had never believed that my mother could be sick outside her own universe. Her little world, it seemed to me, would have helped her to make a recovery. One look at familiar objects must raise the soul. These were probably magical fabrications on my part. Besides, was this woman I saw before me still my mother? A red rash covered her face.

In her eyes I could see that she was apologising for upsetting everybody and for all the bother she was causing us. She wasn't resigned to her fate; that reassured me. I bent down towards her, I heard the word hospital. I thought I could guess what she wanted to say: 'Why in God's name have they put me in hospital?' She had held on to the prejudice against hospitals that is widespread among people living in small villages in the country. I can never understand what shame they feel is attached to it. 'They can look after you best in hospital – they're the experts.'

She closed her eyes. She was happy, perhaps less for herself than for her children who, in placing her in hospital care, had done the right thing.

Each of us has only a little parcel of love to share around. Those working in hospitals, the doctors and nurses, are the impersonal servants of a destiny that hands out health, life or death. They can't afford to let themselves be weighed down by feeling compassion for the patients. Pity would only serve to distract them from their work. Modern medical techniques are more help to patients than human emotion. Those who practise medicine are loyal and yet somewhat inhuman like the determinism of the world, which is always kind if we are capable of hearing its voice, a voice that contains the essence of mercy. Don't become too attached to appearances. Meaning is not contained in daily happenings, but deep within yourself. It was as if I was giving a little sermon to myself; you try to keep your spirits up any way you can. You look for words to express what you're feeling, but words are useless, they have no warmth. Words are for the healthy.

Food poisoning, followed by shock, was the diagnosis given. The words turned around in my head. The rehydratation would go ahead in the normal fashion. The illness came from outside her body, that was some consolation, at least. But it had invaded a tired body; her age obviously played a major part in this inability to resist. The urea was also giving them some cause for concern. I would have liked to stay in the room, follow the struggle that was written on her face, participate in any way I could. But visits were limited in special wards such as these. Anyway, what use was it to be at the bedside of a person who was seriously ill? You really only seek reassurance for yourself by your presence. You hate being there but you can't stand the idea of being somewhere else. At night the patients are the responsibility of the nurses. What if her buzzer didn't work? What if the nurse didn't notice that mother was in difficulty? What if the drip stopped flowing? What if pain made her cry out in the dark? Mother turned her head towards the upturned tube that fed the drip. That was a good sign, it showed she wanted to live, you could see hope in her eyes.

She said, 'If I had not come to hospital I'd never have known how nice the nurses are.'

'Of course they are, mother,' I replied. 'It's not just nuns who are nice, you know.'

She smiled.

After three days of examinations, tests, X-rays, they still hadn't discovered exactly what the problem was. The head doctor was nowhere to be found. 'He's waiting like the rest of us for nature to take its course.' I was assured that he would talk to me as soon as possible. I kept on tormenting them for information. I needed to keep busy. All of a sudden everything became simple – my best friend knew the doctor and he phoned him. He would be at the hospital in an hour. It was Sunday. I concluded that the great medical practitioner couldn't be as bad as all that. He had read some of my books; that was fortunate for me. I barely had enough time to run out to get one of my books and write a dedication: 'To Professor X. who was kind enough to interrupt his weekend for . . .' I would have agreed to any humiliation to help my mother.

The doctor was a serious man with a face that carried the imprint of majesty and power like that of the priest in times gone by. Or was it just the fact that we tend to see doctors in their professional capacity, because they spend their time standing up talking to patients in bed, or surrounded by groups of admiring students, esteemed by nurses and families that look at them with imploring eyes that try to read the verdict in the doctors' demeanour. The religion of life has given way to the religion of eternal life. If doctors ever decided to set up a Church they would rule over the whole world.

He repeated the diagnosis I had already been given – food-poisoning followed by shock. The rehydration seemed to be progressing well. And I thought the rehydration was finished! What was the cause? Difficult to say, it was probably infected cream. The lab was working on this. Why was her face so red? That was nothing, more than likely it was caused by the urea. The kidneys may well have suffered some small damage. No need to be worried. Was I worried, I wondered? The thought came to me that I had just talked about my mother as if she were a mere medical case. Now, however, I was full of wild hope. There would be more Sundays, the table would be set. Quickly, go and phone the others. They'll have to look after the flowers in her garden, the lawn. There is watering to be done. It is vital that she finds everything in pristine order. In the end, you only think about yourself.

On Monday afternoon the professor sent for me. 'If you want to do everything in your power to ensure that your mother gets the best treatment, you should bring her to Nantes.' Nantes was one of the only cities in France, apparently, outside of Paris, that had a dialysis machine. No, her condition had not worsened in any way, but if the urea didn't right itself there was a risk that they wouldn't be able to transport her if the need arose. If I wanted to do everything in my power! Besides, anything was better than waiting. So we got things underway immediately. The hospital authorities were notified – they were expecting us, it would be simple. Professor X. phoned up himself. The ambulance and the nurse were ready to take us. There were more tests to be done before we left. Another X-ray was taken, we had to fill out papers, that was the norm. Eventually they rolled mother through the corridors. I could see her eyes questioning me as she gently shook her head.

The Red Cross ambulance was on its way; there were so many

ambulances interspersed on the road. Before this, an ambulance was only a word, an image. You overlook so much suffering. I now know that ambulances also transport dead people. A young woman in a uniform was driving. She struck me as being a bit dry, starchy. A bossy type of smile appeared briefly, then disappeared. This proved to me that her attention span was very limited. In the back of the ambulance mother was lying down. Beside her was a rather rotund nurse. When I turned around to face her, she looked as if she was sympathetic to my mother's plight. She was new to the job and came from the country. The drip was working: mother's eyes seemed to be watching the leaves on the trees as we sped along. I hadn't seen her looking so well since her illness began. The driver tells me that that happens sometimes; some patients feel better when they're driving about than when they're in hospital. She drove quickly and didn't overuse the brakes. I asked her some questions about her job. It appeared that they had to do a special exam. If they were involved in one accident for which they were held responsible, they lost their job. I had the impression that I was boring her with all these questions about her job. I'd say she was saying to herself, 'Who is this guy? He mustn't be too fond of his mother if all he can do is question me about my job.' If she knew I was a priest the conversation would have been smoother, I'd say she was quite a pious type. She blew her horn lightly but in an imperious manner. At that moment I would have loved to be a helmeted policeman on a motorbike, dressed in black and white, clearing the road of traffic in front of the ambulance so that it could go along at 150 kilometres an hour, take risks. A car was wrapped around a tree – the usual crowd of spectators had gathered round. We didn't stop – you can't save everybody. We've only got a limited amount of love to go round. Anyway, the police had arrived on the scene.

Eventually we arrived at Nantes hospital. 'We're saved, mother! Everything will be set in motion to ensure your recovery.' But the hospital was a veritable labyrinth – the ambulance lost its way in the maze of buildings. It was raining. After driving round and round for ages, just when I was about to get out to look for help, we saw the admissions building. People were coming and going, male and female nurses. They didn't look in our direction. They'd been at this job for too long; they'd seen enough pain and suffering. Everyone had their own clearly defined job. The ambulance was left outside in the wind and rain. The girl from the Red Cross took out papers, mentioned a telephone call made by the Professor in Rennes who had set everything up. Who could have taken that call? They looked around, discussed what had to be done. I heard a voice say, 'Look, you're not in Rennes now. This is Nantes!' The Red Cross girl said, 'And I thought I'd be in Rennes for nine o'clock!' She probably wanted to go to the cinema. Mother would have to have another X-ray before being admitted. The X-rays in Rennes revealed nothing. You could be forgiven for thinking that hospitals are strange places, almost hostile. 'Poor mother, you're going to be shunted away again!' Through the rain that was pouring down the window of the ambulance, a Citroën saloon, I tried to smile at her. She returned my smile. I made an attempt to wave and then, miraculously, she raised her left hand. This is the gesture she'd make through the French windows when I left on Sunday afternoons. With her left hand she'd pull back the curtain and I'd see her face through the humidity that had gathered on the windscreen. She would then raise her right hand in a hesitant manner just as I, having turned the car around, would take off in second gear. I never once put my foot on the accelerator without thinking that this was the last time I'd be seeing her wave goodbye. It was true, it was always the last time. Do all men have such fearful souls buried beneath their haughty exteriors?

So then, we had to do this X-ray if we didn't want to be sent away. There was no point in arguing. Orderlies had to be found. In fact, they needed to be requisitioned if the truth be known. They complained that they weren't on duty any more, that their replacements were late. More X-rays. I could hear mother saying, 'I'm cold'. All she had on was the standard-issue hospital attire. She was used to flannel and wool. All during her hospitalisation I'd hear her say that she was cold. I had brought a shawl and a purple cloak that she liked. Every morning I'd find them folded on the table. 'Let her have her cloak or her shawl around her shoulders,' I said. 'It has positive psychological effects'. I tried to negotiate with the hospital authorities but the rules didn't permit patients to wear shawls. Once more we had to go out into the wind, the rain poured down on us. We put mother on the stretcher in the ambulance. 'Go right, then left. You can't miss it.' Those were the directions we were given. Here we were once more wandering around this huge camp of suffering, looking for the intensive care unit. We got lost once more. Buildings floated indistinctly in the misty rain. We stopped twice, we accosted passers-by who told us, 'Go right, then left, then right.' We were in a maze. The driver looked at her watch. She was definitely going to miss her date now.

In the intensive care unit we had to do everything over again. We tried to reason with them, we took out our papers. Finally, they admitted us. But now the orderlies had disappeared. The nurses baulked at the prospect, it wasn't their job to carry a stretcher. Finally the girl from the Red Cross made a decision. She grabbed the stretcher at one end, I took the other. *Visits not allowed. No children under any circumstances may go beyond this door.* The cry of pain from a patient with kidney failure pierced the air and stayed there for a while, as vivid as red blood, before easing to a dull moan, which was followed in turn by a hissing sound that came from the unfortunate patient's insides. Death was palpable here. Mother's eyes seem to be questioning me about what was happening. She was turned this way, then that, in an effort to get her into the bed. The Red Cross lady then said, 'She'll have to give me back the gown.' Couldn't she take one of the Nantes gowns – a gown for a gown? That seemed fair. No, that's not the way things worked. She wanted her gown back immediately. Poor mother being disturbed again. She said, 'I'm cold.'

I had to leave. No arguing, those were the rules. I was nothing more than a man without a tie accompanying a dying woman. They wouldn't even listen to me. I bent over mother's face. She seemed exhausted, far away. I was hit with the full force of her condition when she said, with her eyes closed, in an almost inaudible voice, 'You haven't eaten yet today. You have to eat before you go to sleep.'

I can see more clearly what misplaced reassurance I first got from these words, which upset me at the same time. It seemed to me to be a good sign that she was worried about me in this way. However, her accent was a cause for concern. She was using the patois of her village when she said *mangê* (eat), *dormi* (sleep), just as she would have pronounced them when she was a child. It was as if, since she hadn't spoken the local patois for a long time, she was becoming once more the young mother who forced her puny child, who was always rushing off somewhere, to eat. Before dying, people revert to the language of their childhood. One night I had been present at the last agony of a foreign woman who had been fatally injured. She had forgotten her own language over the years and spoke French. At the end she started groaning in her Slavic mother tongue. A friend once said to me, 'Before dying, if you talk at all, it's always in the language of your childhood, just as in moments of tenderness and love a woman rediscovers her mother tongue.'

Just as I was going through the door of the intensive care unit a woman's voice called me back: 'Has she got medical insurance?' I hadn't a clue. What difference did that make anyway? It changed everything, apparently. It cost a lot for the treatment in that hospital, thirty thousand francs a day. I had to understand that in the case of people on Social Security, things moved more slowly. It was probably in my interest . . .

'Dont waste any time,' I said. 'Don't worry about the cost.'

All that had gone before might be nothing more than a nightmare. The huge recovery machinery was in place now. They were all there, doctors, nurses, all concerned with the same purpose – that of saving lives. Everything was possible. This is what I said to myself the following morning at the time visitors were allowed to go in. Mother was in the same condition. Did Professor Y. call to see her? They weren't too sure. A voice piped up, 'Professor Y. is in Paris until Thursday, maybe even Friday. He's at a conference, he's giving a report. Everyone knows that.' And what about the intern? He was due to arrive this morning. They tried to get him on the phone, but no luck. Eventually someone said he wouldn't be back till late in the afternoon. But anyway, there was no hurry. They'd have to take blood samples, analyse them, do more X-rays, all that sort of thing. There was no point in telling them that all this information was already in her file. Start from scratch, that seemed to be the principle they employed. They needed a new principle then. There was nothing that could be done when it came to fighting rituals.

At the end of the afternoon the intern still hadn't come. Visiting hours were coming to an end.

'Could you give me a sheet of paper, please,' I say to the nurse. 'I'd like to leave a note for the intern. He could give me a call.'

'Explain what you want to say to him and I'll convey the message,' the nurse replied.

'No, I want to write.'

'That's not the way things are done here,' she said.

'I don't give a damn,' I said. 'I'm doing what isn't the done thing.'

She headed off. I should have put on my Roman collar. There would inevitably have been a few women who would have rushed to my assistance for religious reasons. We don't think of everything at times like these. I was wearing a polo-neck sweater, I must have looked like a handyman. Underneath the bitterness, deep within me, someone was delighted that I had to endure the lot of the poor of this world. It's impossible for me to describe the nurses. All I saw were closed faces. I heard their businesslike tone of voice. It must have been my fault. Everything was taking place in a shadowy world. If I had been a disinterested visitor I would have been able to distinguish one nurse from the next, recognise them. In the end a young woman intervened and brought me a writing pad and an envelope. I would have liked to see the face of the man who was now looking after my mother, hear his voice. I would have liked him to explain to me his hopes and fears, so that I could have a few more words to turn over in my head. I would have liked him to tell me stories. And yet, I knew that I might just as well go for a walk along the banks of the Loire. What must happen would happen in the way that it was supposed to happen. I could neither speed up nor slow down the process.

The nurse who brought me the pad came up to me at the door. She looked guilty. 'It's your mother, after all,' she said. 'I think I would do the same if my mother . . . I wouldn't want to be away from her for a second. She's got such beautiful hair, your mother, not a single white strand. I saw you once on the telly.'

The hospital was suddenly becoming human. I had at least one ally in the place. To think that television has that much power!

I was frightened by the redness of my mother's face. I was told that it was not serious. At Rennes they said that the urea level was causing it. At Nantes, it was just a simple inflammation due to the antibiotics. The nurses had removed her dentures. I could no longer see her face, only an old woman's mask with wrinkles all round the mouth that seemed to have a life of their own, something like caterpillars on a piece of fruit. I thought, they're just the ravages of time, and I was almost happy at finding the apt description. It was no longer my mother's face that I saw before me. When she died, I would see her normal face again. Now all I could see was a defenceless face with eyes that furtively examined the space close to them, then stared straight ahead before closing again. She had been the mother who called out, her voice suffused with worry. A slightly dazzled young boy had bent over to look into her eyes, had thought about her and worried in case anything bad happened to her. She had been as necessary to someone as the air we breathe. I would have liked to show her a picture of my father. Perhaps that would remind her of the bright light she thought she saw the day he had been killed.

I would have liked to know what her eyes were saying to me. Why does the image of the colt, Dinan, who died on the footpath, always keep recurring? The grey watery eyes of my mother, it seemed to me, expressed unbounded surprise, supplication, maybe even reproach. Her gaze went up, up, slid away, started off again, like a bee struggling to escape from inside a window, who goes up and down constantly, or like the eyes of a high-flying bird that has been shot down – he strains his neck forward, looks for the sky and when his eyes turn to the ground they once more seek space on high. At Rennes she had looked at the bottle of glucose, the intravenous tube, and there had been a flicker of hope in her eyes. Now there was nothing but a void. For some inexplicable reason the idea came to me again that if her eyes had been able to rest on the familiar objects of her day-to-day life she would have felt some joy, in much the same way as an old dog goes to smell his favouite armchair and his leash, before collapsing dead on the ground.

The intern adopted a professional tone of voice when addressing me. He outlined the position while pointing to graphics and figures on the wall. It was difficult to undergo a kidney dialysis, especially for a patient as weak as my mother. We'd have to await the results of all the tests, see if the urea was decreasing or increasing, whether it was reaching or going beyond four–tenths. Only then would the risk be worth taking. 'We'll just have to adopt a wait-and-see approach,' he said. He was rather proud of his diagnosis, gaves himself a good mark. I prefer this dry, professional language to kind words. It is better that human sentiment does not get in the way of one's reflexes when it comes to medicine. One sentence spun around in my brain: 'The operation was a success, the patient died.' With that, I imagined hearing the high-pitched laughs of the nurses in the corridors. When they arrived at the door of the patient's room they once more assumed their impersonal mask.

You are not present at your own death. But it is impossible to escape from the death of someone you love. When you write, you love once more, suffer the pain all over again. But enough clever words for now. Why is it that I can't stay still and suffer with dignity? It wasn't the first time that a mother was about to die, after all. Besides, I hardly suffer at all any more, when I am writing. I change the pain into joy. Enough, no more clever words. It would be better to suffer in silence and to metamorphose your suffering in a supernatural manner. And what if I could only achieve that through writing? I am suspicious of angels. I wish people would let me live like an member of the human race.

The nights were difficult. I would wake up ten or twenty times with a start. I thought I could hear the phone ringing, or if it did actually ring, I waited, contorted like a sick animal, while the porter went to answer it. I waited for his footsteps, for him to come and knock on someone's door – it's not our turn yet. On other occasions I saw her face as she lay on the pillow. I caught myself breathing like she did. I had to make a big effort to catch my breath again – I must have been training for death. I suddenly felt in my muscles the desire to jump out of bed, to run to the hospital and hold her hand. I would be thrown out. There are billions of men and women who have known nights of panic like these, who will have to endure worse.

Although I was all alone in this city, I did have friends from the worlds of literature and cinema. They weren't very Catholic in the strict sense of the word, nor were they proud of what they were. I respected them for that. All I had to do was pick up the phone.

Shame prevented me from doing this, I wasn't up to it. The old priestly pride was still there. If I'm not capable of presenting a good image of myself, whether it has to do with faith or expressing indignation, I just hide. Now, if I was to break down in their presence, then I might be of some help to them.

What an unrelenting summer. If only it would rain or get windy, if the sky would only have the decency to cloud over. The city looks like it is boiling up behind the cloud of fog that separates me from it. Cars, like lemmings, rush headlong towards the ocean. I am ashamed to be walking among tourists, ashamed of going into a restaurant while my dried up lips unconsciously form silent groans and my mind goes back to that awful moan I heard the first evening in the intensive care unit – it sounded exactly like an animal who was being slowly bled to death. The moan rose up, up, almost in a straight horizontal line. I'm just a leper among the living. People stare at my face like flies swarming around a bowl of fruit. Puppets are moving around on a frozen stage. Transient humans come and go, inspired to persevere by a strength that is not in them, that has to be coming from outside their bodies. There is a time for birth, a time to live in innocence, a time to feel death assailing you from beneath, a time for death. There is a time for throwing stones, a time for picking them up. Mother, I would have loved to hide you with your imminent death, like you hide a forbidden love. The faces became indistinct, faded under the too bright light – all these living creatures who looked so proud, with their pouches and tubes, their organs, tumours, which carry life, death or illness. People in mourning everywhere. Shop windows displayed wreaths, crucifixes in genuine bronze. I came across hearses everywhere, undertakers walking beside them, or in cars, soutanes: *requiescant in pace.* And always there were these tourists sniffing around with their enormous snouts, insatiable when it comes to tragedy, with their binoculars, lenses. Couldn't they just mind their own business!

I headed to a restaurant on the Place du Commerce, a dodgy enough place frequented by salesmen. At least it had the advantage of taking me away from those awful tourists. I just needed to be fortified with glucose – I wasn't hungry. There were all types of hors d'oeuvres, chateaubriand steak, vanilla pralines, muscadet wine. All around me people were drinking, eating and laughing. The waitress wiggled her hips and they were frozen for a second like when a film uses the freeze-frame, then they started up their conversation once more. There's a time to laugh, a time to cry.

There was a man on his own at a table, tears running down his face without his even seeming to realise it. A stranger approached, put his hand on the man's shoulder. They left the restaurant together. The man told him everything – his mother, the hospital. The stranger remained silent. All this was a figment of my imagination but it was this type of stranger I would have liked to meet in my present state. Strangers can be our best friends. It must have been the glass of muscadet that brought this on, or fatigue.

I thought, Oh God, if you had the power you're reputed to have, you couldn't be absent from our suffering, humble God; you are only distant so that you can enlarge our hearts perpetually. I don't want anyone else to tell me about your omnipotence; it's your weakness I adore, like when Herod was following you, when the Pharisees were tracking you down, when the soldiers nailed you to the Cross. I know no other God than the Son of Man. I have no questions to put to you. It's the life You give us that asks the questions. When my moment comes, help me to answer correctly. It must have been the muscadet I drank that had me in this state.

The hospital was outside the city, beyond the river. There were three bridges on the first section of the river. After that, the cars all converged on the only bridge on the second section of the river, the diabolical Pirmil bridge. Cars were bumper to bumper. Ten feet every three minutes, in a cloud of carbon monoxide, under the relentless sun.

It's a bit better now, I was told. But there's a bit of an obstruction around the . . . Her temperature has gone up, gone down. She's not as tired as she was yesterday. She's more tired, yes, she's very tired. They were very skilled at using euphemisms in this place. One evening I found that her buzzer was disconnected. The nurse merely said to me, 'These things happen.'

People were born here, died, hoped, despaired, amidst the comings and goings of this hospital that resembled a city. There were happy

106

people in front of the buildings, they were full of life. There were others in tears. I think the staff there worked three eight-hour shifts: the different teams of nurses crossed each others' paths at the beginning or end of shifts, they called out to one another, laughed, wished each other a nice weekend, or happy holidays . . . 'I'm heading to Spain.' 'I'm going to the Alps.' Those recovering from accidents tried their first steps along the lawns.

The probe they inserted was causing mother to cry out in pain. White saliva changed into a crust, almost cemented her lips together like plaster. I thought that she wanted to speak, but I could only hear indistinct and incomprehensible sounds. Once more I headed off to look for a nurse.

'I hear you, sir. We're doing everything in our power to help your mother.'

All she wanted to do was defend the institution.

'I envy your being close to my mother. Would you have pity on her at least for my sake?'

My words made no impression whatsoever on her. A sudden realisation struck me: the nurses are not assigned to specific patients. Everyone was responsible and no one was. That's why I was coming up against a wall. The one who told me mother had beautiful hair had gone.

A scarlet face, eyes that blindly scrutinised the space around her, caked saliva around the dried-up lips, this is the image of my mother I had to bring with me across the city.

I thought I was a well-organised person. I suppose I had succeeded in exercising some control over my thoughts. When you eliminate the images of the past, the future, you are left with great peace of mind. Our pain and suffering are only the consequence of how attached we are to ourselves. Now the dams have been pierced and I don't want any more of this stupid joy. I implore him who represents Divine Hope: *Out of the depths I cry to You, O Lord.* As mother could no longer pray for herself I lent her my voice. When images hurt me, when the teeth of memory dig into my heart, I sometimes murmur, 'Our Lady of Lourdes, pray for us.' Does such a prayer ever reach Heaven? I couldn't yet resign myself to say, 'Save my mother!' Let what is to happen

happen but just grant that I have the strength to accept it. I had the impression that deep down within me, beneath all my abstract ruminations, an almost inaudible voice was saying, 'Thy will be done.'

I thought I was an adult. Maturity has nothing to do with age. My serenity was merely a defence mechanism that I was using to hide my fear. I had seen people die, I had come very close to death myself on two separate occasions. I thought I knew something about it but I knew nothing at all.

It is much better to say goodbye to those you love long before their last hour comes. You should say it to them when they're in good health; in that way you come to see them differently, in a better light. When you do it that way, everything isn't couched in artificiality. Everything is just appearances now, Sulivan. Wait till the show is over.

It is said that the Christian suffers less because he believes. That's just one more magical fabrication of our faith. Heaven, the next world, these are only words for me. I find it impossible to form an image in my mind of what they represent. The world is not merely made up of land, water and light, but also of darkness. In the same way, faith is not only light, but also darkness. Everything that succeeds in making inroads on selfishness, power, pride, everything that is transformed into real love, that is what heaven is about. 'You will meet her again in Heaven'. I don't know what that means. I do have the conviction that there is such a thing as an eternal presence, but it in no way alleviates the heartbreak I'm feeling, *hic et nunc.*

I thought I had some knowledge of the world; I latched on to God in the same way as others give themselves over completely to art, to love. I should have been less proud. The same words can hide the same fear. I used to say the word 'Joy', but this simply described a human joy I had made for myself. My footsteps were like a hymn for peace in my heart. I believed that all my days would only be hard and brilliant pearls of immense value. Quite simply, I hadn't a clue what life was all about; I followed the instinctive probings of my soul, I fed off my own fervour. It was only now I was being asked the hard questions.

Anticipate every goodbye, I said to myself. Because how can we escape the destiny that comes to us from a foreign source if not by transforming this destiny within ourselves? If I accept the death of what I love, I am only being disloyal to life, out of loyalty to the ultimate meaning of life. I thus become invulnerable. It is in this way that Jesus asks his friends to leave their fathers, mothers, brothers and sisters in order for them to surpass the destiny that weighs down our human body. If someone asks you to to travel a short distance with him, go a longer distance. If someone steals your tunic, give him your overcoat as well – it is in this way that we come to know what freedom is. God, I'm trying to push myself. A feeling of invulnerability is also a temptation. Hope in you alone might detach me from this world as the rising sap of spring removes the last dead leaves from the trees. Rational thoughts will be of no use to me as they are nothing but a protection we give ourselves against fear.

Churches are still a refuge for the unfortunate members of society. They seek shelter there from the heat, the cold, the noise. Before setting out on the dreaded road to the hospital I went to bury myself in the church in Nantes, what was it called again? I can't remember. It was such a beautiful place, probably the last church left where vespers are still sung in Latin. In the middle of the city, full of summer holiday-makers, on this Sunday, I discovered something had been preserved from my childhood. The Latin floated through the air:

In exitu Israel de Egypto . . .
Manus habent et non palpabunt
Pedes habent et non ambulabunt
Oculos habent et non videbunt . . .

It is in this way that Scripture talks about idols. The voices from the choir in the gallery floated down over the heads of about twenty women who were kneeling in different parts of the church. My mother dragged me off for years to Sunday vespers. I recognised the words, the smell of the incense. Now I felt grateful to her for having forced me into this devotion. The women in the church now were like those in our church at home, those eternal saintly women. Women of their generation hadn't to endure advertising for 'super-girdles' that make you look and feel thinner, creams to keep you young-looking, all these images that assail us nowadays and trivialise life and make everything appear superficial. The daring luxury of the cities, the gimmicks that are meant to make your life easier, didn't invade their consciousness at all – they grew old peacefully without worrying about their youth deserting them. They hadn't the time to see themselves change over the years. It seemed to me now, all of a sudden, that there was more truth in the stillness of this one church than in the mad activity of the whole city.

These women were believers, alone, enduring everything, they had to face up to men who insisted on being commonsensical in their approach to life, even hard, to children who seemed deaf and selfish at times – determined women who tried to get both their husbands and children to follow the virtuous path. Such women seem so defenceless with their simple language, their derisory pious images, habits from another age. Yet they never admit defeat, they're capable of loving despite the hardships, always patient, always ready to believe in what is good, not even aware that they are actually sacrificing themselves. I would also like to sing a song of praise to the good people in the world, I would like to sing a hymn to a woman so like these elderly insignificant women attending Sunday vespers, a service that is surely destined to soon fall into disuse.

My mother had no religion any more. Already, in Rennes, when I showed her the crucifix on the wall, she would turn her head away. She refused to take the rosary beads that had never left her side throughout her life. 'This is a good time,' I said, 'to invoke Our Lady of Lourdes.' When I did so I could clearly see a small smile forming, first in her eyes and then around her mouth. I had habitually teased her about her pious devotions – she obviously hadn't forgotten. The smile told me as much. But immediately after this, she shook her head once more, raised her free hand, let it fall again and went, No! No! I said to myself that a sentimental type of religion, preoccupied with emotion, stayed on the surface of things. Acceptance and refusal of God went on at a much deeper level. Just as her house, her garden, even her children, might mean nothing to her and the many daily worries might be shed like an old skin, in the same way the God to whom she was too close and whom she was invoking now, the divine object she used to console herself, seemed to have deserted her. But in the unseen part of her soul she was still attached to the living and true God. Nature restricts our field of vision at the same time as the space we occupy in a narrow room. She was just totally taken up with the struggle to survive. I consoled myself with such thoughts. I saw them as a good sign, they eased my worry about her possible loss of faith for a while. In the same way, I was consoled those first days when she'd constantly say, 'What time is it? The time seems to be going by very slowly. 'Her will to live is still strong,' I thought. ' She already wants to put this illness behind her.'

In Nantes that day, when I once more talked to her about God, she was no longer able to move her hand, but she still shook her head. The certainty suddenly struck me, with the force of a stab from a sharp knife, that she was already very far from us, in that zone where words and simple pieties are of no use. Only at that precise moment did I know that she was going to die, that she was replacing Christ on the naked cross, experiencing all the feelings of abandonment. I could see her eyes – I couldn't, I wouldn't read what they were saying. I would only know later.

Maurice had now arrived. I had sent him a telegram telling him to come back by train. Naturally enough, he didn't listen to my advice. He came back from Alicante by driving non-stop, day and night. The first morning that we saw her together, I found her a little bit better. Maurice was the youngest in the family. We often teased mother about him being the pet. I said, 'Maurice is here.' She made an attempt to smile and then said, 'You came back from your holidays on account of me.' She seemed apologetic. When we left the hospital we were almost what you'd call happy. She had been getting hard of hearing lately – we'd buy her a hearing aid. We planned how we'd install a call-button near her bed at home. We wouldn't bother with a phone, we decided, it wasn't enough to meet her needs. After all, if you were very sick you'd have to drag yourself over to it. We were trying to reassure each other. I wasn't able to really enter into the spirit of things, however. I had forgotten how to play such games. Maurice turned to me at one point and said, 'You speak as if she were already . . .' 'Yes, it's strange,' I said. 'Even before this happened I was surprised to find myself writing about her in the past tense.'

111

I was driving to the house. This was the first time that she would not be waiting for me there. Mother was dead.

The phone had rung at around eleven o'clock in the morning. They had had to raise the bed because, as she was unable to swallow her saliva any more, she was choking. So that was why her head was facing downwards when I arrived. But, her gaze went up and up like a bee trapped inside the window, falling, then rising again, without seeing anything, or like the eyes of high-flying birds. Professor Y., who had finally arrived back from his conference, said that there was no more hope, that we could bring her home if we wanted to. How quickly things can go from hope to despair. I asked for the chaplain to administer her a simple form of extreme unction – it had already been done apparently, the chaplain had called in to see her yesterday evening. Everything followed a set pattern in that hospital. When mother was put in the ambulance to bring her home, just as the drip was put in place, she died. The nurse stayed beside her until we reached the hospital exit. The driver said, 'What we're about to do is a bit irregular but, with a bit of luck, we won't get caught. No, don't close her eyes.' I didn't understand why her eyes should be left open. And so, all during the journey, the images of the sky were reflected in her eyes, as they are in nature. I got out of the ambulance. A messenger is always needed to convey bad news.

And now here I was driving towards the house in a state of desolation. To whom could I talk? I still thought I was going to her to tell her about my woes. It's crazy, I know. Slow down for God's sake . . . Suddenly I experienced something approaching a moment of relief from my suffering. Once more the same thought came back: you are absent from your own death, never from the death of those you love. My death was now behind me. Ivan Illitch, after having endured so many terrors, is amazed because he is no longer afraid. 'What joy,' he says, 'there is no such thing as death anymore.' I would have loved for mother to have had this insight. I felt it myself for a second on this road, long enough for me to retain a vivid image of it in my mind. I thought I had seen in the past the eyes of dying people flowing towards eternity like water to a spring. All mother's eyes expressed were emptiness and abandon. The thought came to me that in dying she

112

had given me a lesson, to me who had given so many of them to others, a frightening lesson the exact meaning of which I didn't yet dare to contemplate.

If someone loves me enough, I said to myself, to take my wishes seriously, I want nobody besides the medical specialists to be present at my death. It is frightening to show this spectacle to any living person.

The garden had never been such a riot of colour. The pink, red and yellow petunias were coming over the edges of the paths.

When we got her out of the ambulance, her face had the horrible grimace of death. Her tongue was caught between her lips. I put her tongue back in, smoothed her lips and closed her eyes. The gestures we make at times like these are strange, as if there is some ancient wisdom within us that knows better than we do. Someone went to get the nuns from the boarding school adjoining our house. They said that they didn't usually prepare corpses for burial, but they'd make an exception for mother, who was a saint, and for me, a priest. I wasn't to tell anyone about it. They brought everything they needed – candles, holy water, a sprig. They put a crucifix standing up near the bed. Mother had had everything ready for her death for a long time, she had put the materials in the wardrobe behind a pile of sheets. I had forgotten about this. I went out for a walk among the flowers and a sudden idea pierced my heart – those she loved, who were now dead, my father, her parents, will no longer exist in anyone's memory. So many links that had been built up between the various faces, between places that enabled people to exist together in the memory of someone's heart, will now be as though they had never existed.

An hour later when I came back into the room, her face was once more like that of her youth, surrounded by her thick hair. She seemed to be totally focused on some inner conviction. Such was her concentration that she came across as being in some way serious or solemn, yet behind it all could be seen the gentle smile of the person who has discovered knowledge. This face reminded me of something – yes, it was this face that I'd seen as a child when I was beside her in the church and I'd watched her pray. The thought struck me that prayer and death are related in some way. The face was also the one

113

from the picture that I had triumphantly, and misguidedly, brought down from the attic one Sunday afternoon. There was something more knowing about her face in death, however, as if it had taken a full and long life to tell her . . . what exactly?

This smile, which was slightly self-satisfied, maybe even discreetly ironic, like one sometimes sees when a person is thinking of something that they can't reveal to anyone else, was a sign. In this face, I said to myself, is contained the meaning of a whole life. Then I thought of the last line of one of Yeats's books which had struck a chord with me: *Life is just a long preparation for something that never happens.* But something does happen, I thought. All the nervous stress leaves your body. You become totally relaxed in death. We are all blind thinking that life consists of possessing material goods, holding onto this, then that, getting to know one thing, then another, trying desperately to ignore the fact that the whole process inevitably amounts to absolutely nothing. Life isn't just a game where you have to possess and know as many things as possible. Rather, it is about reducing yourself to zero, living in a new and more authentic way. And all life's meaning suddenly became clear to me: you have to always put yourself last, be there for others. But once more I realised that I was using ideas to keep my mind busy, to suffer less.

Don't get too carried away, the ironic voice inside me said. 'You know perfectly well what her face was like when you arrived home in the ambulance. Rigor mortis is the explanation for the furtive smile, the look of peace.' But whatever it was, that smile moved me in the same way as a promise.

In the presbytery the parish priest asked if we wanted the 'best' funeral available. I said, 'Yes, the best,' without thinking. He said that unfortunately we would not be able to have the solemn ringing of the bells because one of them wasn't working. That's the problem when the bells are worked by electricity. If he only knew how completely indifferent I was to the bell that didn't work, to the 'best' funeral Mass available. An ordinary low Mass, one evening at nightfall or one morning at dawn would have done me. Afterwards, we could have driven my mother to the valley of Jehoshaphat, with just a few friends, her sons, her daughter. That would have been just right. At the same time I see that the poor parish priest is genuinely saddened at the death of my mother. He says, 'Soon I'll have no one in the church for daily mass. Your mother was in the church every morning.'

I have spent two days coming and going from mother's room to the garden, from the garden to her room. The petunias are really growing over onto the paths. I have never seen the rhododendrons flower so brilliantly as they have done this year. The dahlias, however, are falling down and need stakes to keep them upright. The pots containing the chrysanthemums are in their usual place under the shed. She used to always think about the chrysanthemums. Would they flower for the first of November? There's no point now in removing the stones, the hoses used for watering the flowers and the grass, the pieces of wire that were lying around. I had been afraid that she would break her hip-bone. It's always something you don't expect that ends up happening. Still, it's better to tidy things away; somebody else could fall and get hurt. I force myself into action. Kind thoughts like this are somewhat foreign to me. I tidy things away, I prune, I water just like my mother would have done. 'You must have great faith,' people say to me. If they only knew that this is the last time I will walk in this garden and prune and water. But what is to prevent faith from expressing itself also through our defence mechanisms? In reality my heart is as hard as a stone. I console those who are crying in a cold, aloof manner. In moments when I was in extreme danger I don't think I ever showed any sign of emotion, while in daily life I often feel like a coward. It's the same with my mother's death. The funeral was all about appearances. I had said goodbye a long time ago. How strange it is to see these hands stretched out to me in sympathy: 'We're sorry for your troubles, Father.' I will hold out until the curtain falls. Then the two of us will be alone, mother. I will bring you off with me, you will follow me everywhere. People must think that I am very dispassionate. A bishop in his full violet-coloured apparel came to the house. I introduced him to the family.

'Mother would have been so pleased to be visited by the Church triumphant,' I said.

They laughed through their tears.

'You amaze me,' said Maurice. 'You don't appear to be . . .'

'No, I got all that mourning behind me a long time ago, and it will hit me again in the future. It's almost as if what's going on now doesn't concern me.'

I felt completely empty, almost as if I had been subjected to hours toiling under a scorching sun.

On the eve of the funeral the sacristan brought a huge copper crucifix, which he placed near mother's bed. Then he threw a big bundle of black funeral drapes into the room, raising a cloud of dust. I made him put the whole lot in another room as quickly as possible. I would have liked to be spared the black cloth draped around the coffin, the black drapes. And then there were those silly silver tears that would be hung on the door of the house. You always have someone who'll say, 'What will people think? They'll talk and wonder why we don't do things the same way as everyone else.' And then there is the supreme argument to which there is no comeback: 'Your mother would have liked to follow conventions in this matter.' Anyway, what difference does it make? Words come to my throat, I'd like to explain to them, say that signs are important, that the struggle for a style is the same as the struggle for eternal life. The coffin draped in black, all the frills, the procession, all these faces expressing sadness, the limp hands extended in sympathy: 'So sorry, Father. You have my sincere, my heartfelt, my genuine expression of condolence,' – all this is done in an attempt to suggest the opposite to what our faith proclaims through the words of the liturgy. I would like to flee far away, walk among the trees, listen to Bach; she would be present to me then. The traditional rituals associated with death only want one thing – to eliminate as quickly as possible the suffering of those who are still alive, to expel the dead from this life for once and for all in a flood of tears.

The sky has at last closed in on her. Mother would be happy in the earth. There are no more seasons for her now. We don't have to worry on her account any more about whether it's raining, hot or cold.

The parish priest came at nightfall for the wake. I expected the worst. I was afraid that he might use death as a means of warning the living. My mother had more friends than I thought; they couldn't all fit into the room. Many of them were crying. Then again, they could have been crying for all those who had died belonging to them. The priest had a deep voice that was tinged with emotion and very humble. He wasn't interested in teaching anyone a lesson and seemed to be talking to himself. He read some Psalms, the passage in the Gospel about Lazarus. The texts he chose spoke about the after-life, angels. For a long time such images didn't hold my attention any more than they did my mother's. But I thought about my brothers who lived in the cities. The afterlife – you'd need to tell them that the afterlife, the hereafter, is not a place, nor is eternity a time outside of time. The hereafter is here, that is, beyond the mindless desire to take, to amass material possessions, it is in love that is not simply desire, in love that seeks eternity. Where did I get this obsession to use again the ideas that are common parlance among people of my acquaintance? I'll have to tell them tomorrow after the . . . We will take a meal together as if she were still among us. I would have liked the Mass to be a meal without any spectators, something simple among brothers and sisters who join in the breaking of the bread. That will happen some day – the Mystery will cease to be a spectacle. I'll have to endure the ceremony, listen to the music: *dies irae, dies illa.* It doesn't matter! I'll also put up with that pain. Afterwards I will try to tell them how to live in the afterlife without worrying too much about heaven.

I was more attached to the body than I thought. We are forever trying to fool ourselves. When the undertakers came to take the coffin away I faltered. I escaped out among the flowers in the garden. Was this cowardly on my part? I didn't want to have proof that she had gone. While the people who deal with death were doing their business, I saw mother's gestures as she waved goodbye for the last time. This was as the rain was falling and she was in the ambulance, in front of the hospital admissions section; the same goodbye as every Sunday. There was only ever one goodbye.

What a burden it is to describe how I felt! Language is crushing at times – you get tired trying to manipulate it so that it will express exactly what you want it to. 'Sincere, my genuine, heart-felt sympathies.' I've *lost* my mother and they say they're sorry. I'd like to shout at them that you never *lose* anyone, that my mother was never so alive. But what purpose would that serve?

If you had died in India, mother, on leaving the house we would have turned your coffin around three times. This is because in India it is important that the dead lose all trace of their former paths and that they head off down the great final road of eternity without any thought of turning back. We would have brought you to the edge of the river on your funeral pyre, and I, being the eldest in the family, would have waded into the water until it was up to my chest, holding on my left shoulder the urn containing your ashes. Then, standing still and and without turning around, holding the urn with my two hands, I would have dispersed your ashes behind my back. If I had done that, I think you would have been more present, because the thought of your smile as a young girl, now that you are dead and buried in the ground, in those horrible varnished planks of wood, would separate me less from you.

When the funeral cortège had formed, at the moment when we were about to leave the house to head for the church, in the midst of the loud ringing of the church bells, tears started to roll down my cheeks and I had the sudden impression that I was giving a good impersonation of the grieving son. I could have let myself go, taken pleasure in the images evoked by my tears, or else I could just empty myself of all emotion and become like a vacuum. I decided, or something decided for me, to keep the pain hidden deep within me and not to waste it by giving in to appearances. I masked myself behind a pair of dark glasses and went forward stiffly like an important official carrying out a social function.

Mother thought that a priest should never cry. She had long believed also that he had complete control over sadness, that all he'd have to do, for example, in the case of a fire, was to raise his hand in benediction for the fire to stop. She thought that this power was linked to the priestly function. Poor mother probably always believed a bit too much in the natural power of faith. She herself had been crucified on the naked cross before dying. She had known the abandon that mercy preserves for those it loves.

Now the phone can ring all night as far as I'm concerned. I feel a joy tinged with sadness when I say to myself that there's nothing to worry about any more. This is a mistake because mother dies every night, as if everything happens outside of the time that is measured by clocks.

I had felt that Paris would help me. But even in my apartment on the avenue Montaigne, memories of mother's simple house come back to haunt me – me, who had thought myself so organised, an intellectual, the master of images . . .

> *Et la mort entre en moi*
> *Comme dans un moulin*
> *La mort visable boit et mange*
> *A mes dépens.* *

The roses, sent to me by readers as an expression of sympathy before I've had time to react to mother's death, are thrown in the bin. Sometimes, if I allow myself to wander along the flea market, the tears start flowing at the sight of the various odds and ends. I know it's silly – I see old hands holding lamps, winding grandfather clocks and they remind me of my mother's hands.

Watching television is also dangerous. All I need to start me off is a few images of war, all those soldiers jumping around on the old newsreels, just like puppets making silly gestures, before they're cut down. A shudder takes hold of my whole body and I feel very dizzy before an obscure thought becomes suddenly clear: I have the shattering intuition that my father is well and truly dead now because no one, since mother's eyes were closed for the last time, now has the image of him in their mind. So it is almost as though he had never existed. I couldn't really say that this is a feeling that is unique to me. My father's death didn't really impact positively or negatively on me. Everything happens inside me almost in spite of me.

---

* And death enters my life, / As if into a mill, / Visible death eats and drinks, / At my expense

Despite the rituals surrounding the death of my mother, I had gone into a protective shell. The shell has now cracked. The worn steps of a house, the rain, the dry weather, a clock, the word *manger*, the word *mère*, especially flowers, forsythia, petunias, rhododendrums . . . all these things cause me pain, the pain of memory and association. And even if I am able overcome the images during the day, at night they come at me like a funeral cortège, unrelentingly.

When you dream you are buried in the ground while still conscious, as though you are unjustly condemned to never sleep again, is that like dreaming you are in hell? It was me in that dream and at the same time it wasn't me. I find it impossible to express my sense of anguish at this. When I tried to cry out, no sound would issue from my mouth. I could see mother's smile under the ground.

I am now the son of nobody. I will have to go alone now, mother, like an adult, towards my maker. You were a sign that He existed; I knew through you of His presence. But I was probably too close to you to recognise what was happening. Now that you are gone, mother, there is nothing else between me and death, that is to say between me and God. Alleluia. Who is that inside me saying this word, Alleluia?

A friend gave me the key of his country house to allow me to be alone with the death of my mother. I'll stay there right until the end of the summer. These will be my last months of 'rural civilisation'! Mother was my only home, my sole refuge. The only evidence of the earth in my future abodes will be contained in a few pots of flowers on a balcony. What does it matter! The universe belongs to me. If I am allowed the time, that is to say if God, the source of life, is to grant me enough time, I think I will race around the world – less to see than to meet people – and through my writings push back the boundaries of prejudice. India, China – I'd really like to go there – North and South America, South Africa – before the whole thing explodes over there – these are the places I'd like to visit. Ever since the Russian astronauts, Spudniks, by enlarging human boundaries, showed us the limits we can achieve, we know a little bit better that salvation won't come from outside, but from the unexplored depths of man and of the Son of

Man. Mother, you will follow me wherever I go. I will struggle with your religion, for it and against it. We have not finished our conversation about religious matters yet.

What madness inspired me to stay alone in this house? It seemed to me that all distractions would be a sacrilege against mother's memory and that I needed to endure torment, the gnawing memories that would form in my head, to wait for some obscure type of essence to be revealed, maybe that secret joy that lies ready in us, beneath all the layers of our soul.

The 'château', as the house my rich friend owns is called, overlooks and lies very close to the river. In the distance, beyond the river, you can see the green of a large meadow, which is interrupted by the shadow of poplar trees. Then there are green square fields, some others are white with the maturing wheat, others more light coloured with oats, or yellow with rape-seed. You can make out the dark brown fields that have been freshly ploughed, the grey of the dry land, and here and there the slate roofs that look like puddles of water in the light. This mosaic of fields extends as far as the line of a ridge, alongside which runs a path, so that passers-by look as though they have their heads in the air, and through the large bay-windows the countryside seems to drop back towards me or else fall away according to the movements of my body or my angle of vision. It's like a frozen vista, seen from a plane, when the pilot manipulates the wing to swoop downwards and then climbs again, tests the space around him and then chooses the direction he wishes to go. It's just a question of turning your head a few degrees to the left, as long as you lower your eyes, and there is the mill, the large black wheel, which explains the loud noise of the water being splashed and churned about; on the right you have the high poplars, which are always fluttering in the breeze, the spray of water which seems to surge into the air along the river.

The herd of animals in the large meadow come and go like the tide: they head to the right to graze, forming brown or white or black spots superimposed on the green of the grass. At midday you can no longer see the herd behind the poplars, but they come back around evening time.

I have to be careful of every gesture I make here. Words now resound in my head that I don't recall hearing before. Take, for example, my problems with some gadget or other. Mother's words come back to me: 'Always turn off the gas, don't just check the particular ring that you've been using, I read in the newspaper . . . Steaks can be dangerous – only leave them on the pan for ten seconds on either side, that's enough. Your sister-in-law told me that ten years ago. My generation were never taught anything. I had to wait until I was sixty-five years of age to learn. All my life I have eaten steaks and given them to guests to eat that were as tough as nails . . . Be careful with artichokes. After boiling them don't throw the water from the saucepan into the sink. It's the best weed-killer I know, I read it in *La Croix*.'

Night-time is also risky. At dusk I walk along the roads. The farms are spread out, there's a good distance between each one. I can make out the figure of a woman at the end of a courtyard. Her voice is full of panic:

'Is that you?'

'No, Madame.'

'Oh God, oh God, you haven't by any chance come across an accident? Sometimes he . . .'

It's the same everywhere you go. My mother used to come to the side of the road like that, waiting for my step-father to come home. A dog barks, another answers; suddenly there are ten, a hundred of them barking in unison. What's to stop all the dogs between here and the sea joining in this barking? There are some large birds in the trees, I can hear the croaking of the frogs, the one short utterance of a toad. Some other animal is jumping, another fleeing; there's a skirmish, then a cry – an animal must have been injured. There are a thousand indistinct rustling sounds in the grass, a myriad of noises that you can barely guess at, inaudible to the human ear. It's like the flowers in the short story about an American who invented a machine to capture and translate the shouts of ecstasy that flowers emit when they open up, the screams of roses when they are cut. And then of course there are those cameras, not imaginary this time, constructed by man, which are capable of registering, of reproducing, of translating the heretofore unknown language of the deep ocean – the calls, the shouts of joy, the groans of the dolphins, for example, those dogs of the sea. If I possessed a superhuman hearing faculty I would hear everywhere screams of rage and love intermingled, of hope and despair. I would live all my life in a battlefield. And if God possesses such a hearing faculty, what a symphony must rise up from the earth – the soft sound of the flute to express serenity, the deep wounds captured by the oboe, scepticism by the bassoon, lightheartedness by the trumpet, distress by the saxaphone, the perils of death by the cymbals, the shouts that are needed to give birth and to die, the wails of all men, of all animals on earth, beneath it and in the sky, and other cries, maybe, in other worlds and in galaxies without number would be captured by the roll of the drum . . . Mother, how inadequate is the voice of our agony and how impoverished is my song!

Lights come on in the windows of the farmhouses. I'd like to knock on a door, go in, sit down in the warmth of a family without making any fuss. Come on, Sulivan, you know well that you wouldn't last more than a quarter of an hour. All these farms are like Fontaines noires. The same to-ing and fro-ing in the yards, at night the long shadows made by the lamps on the walls, the creaking of the chains, the sound of the animals rubbing up against the timber stakes to scratch themselves, the noise of straw being crushed under the animals' hooves, a colt running wildly about the yard, mother terrified on the doorstep as the men try to capture it, the healthy smell of manure – I think I can still even differentiate between the smell of horse, cow, pig and rabbit dung. There's some sort of confab going on at the door of one of the sheds. The vet must be here; there's a Mercedes in front of the house. There's a lot more than the fear of losing money to be read in mother's worried expression. The colt was part of the family. This is the reason why she locked herself in the house when any of the animals was being taken away. It would take her hours to get over her pain. Of course, she'd never admit anything of the sort. You were such a frightened, sensitive person, mother.

'I couldn't let on what I was feeling. I had to be silent. Nobody would have . . . You're not making fun of me anymore are you, son? I have the impression that you're listening to me now . . . After all, these animals gave us their milk, they worked in our fields, they each had a name that described their character, their little idiosyncracies. Do you remember Charmante, Décidée, Barbichette, Jegado? Nowadays they only get numbers, no names. Soon they will be slaughtered and made into steaks in the factories. And do you remember Dinan, the colt? And our dogs who died of old age and whom I pretended to chase away? I can tell you now that I used to secretly give them scraps to eat.'

'We knew that, mother.'

'You knew it and said nothing, you devils! Do you know why I don't want either a dog or a cat now? I can tell you: I'm afraid of losing them. It's as simple as that. Do you think that these are feelings that I have the right to have? And there's one more thing I want to ask you: since men rise from the dead, why couldn't animals do the same? Do you have the right to wish for the resurrection of animals? Does the Church . . . ?'

'You have the right, mother. You have the right to think and do anything you wish. You are now reigning with God in heaven.'

I know all this reminiscing is sentimental, a bit melodramatic. It's not the first time that someone's mother has died. I don't care about that. Writing down these little anecdotes, expressing ordinary feelings, which quite possibly millions of people secretly feel after seeing their own mother dying, reassures and comforts me a bit. It sometimes seems to me that my mother is the humble mother of a great number of people.

I think that I am forcing myself to look, to listen, to dream, to fall asleep so that I won't see these images any more, nor hear anything that I will have to explain. One night I saw her eyes: the black pupils, the iris grey with water but becoming white at the end of the dark circle that marks the beginning of the cornea. It was as if nothingness was invading the warmth of life itself. The worst part was the knowledge that my mother hadn't accepted death. She had protected herself all during her life with words, religious practices. She had had all the feelings of piety, of resignation, of knowing God's love, but she hadn't been able to accept the reality of death. In the hospital at Nantes I had had a brief insight into this but had pushed it to the back of my mind. Mother had known abandon. Her eyes were screaming, 'Why did you make us mortal?'

It was obvious to me that night. Was I dreaming or awake? I was on my deathbed with the same questioning look on my face as my mother had had. I no longer knew if I was my mother, myself, another, all humanity. A cry rose up from the heart of life. I got out of bed, I was crying, 'Why did you make us mortal?' I had all the answers up there in my head, all the philosophy, all the certainties of religion that I imparted to my congregation, but the tears were still flowing from all the eyes of those who were mortal. They were asking, 'Why did you make us mortal?' The ideas were intact but that night they were no good to me. I would return to them the next day but for the moment all I could do was cry out in the darkness.

I would like to know if dead people communicate with one another. Really, I shouldn't use the term dead people; survivors would be more accurate because if they live they are more alive than we are, and the dead only die to those whom they leave in this world and very little to themselves. 'If they live?' Yes, I know, I'm falling over myself with these words, my friends. I believe that Christ rose from the dead, that the dead will rise also, but when it comes to my mother, the image of her face buried under the earth stops me in my tracks. Are you scandalised by such an attitude in a priest? Do you want me to edify you with lies? I want more than anything to believe in eternal life. Are you satisfied with that, you righteous people? If a bullock wants grass it's because there is grass around somewhere. It's the same with a man who is looking for a woman; he believes that there is a woman for him somewhere. And if the spirit is capable of infinite passion, if love wants eternity . . . And don't start thinking that I am going to provide you with proof for all these theories. I have no other proof apart from the Word that leaves us in our misery. When the Son of Man, who is also the Son of God, cries out that he has been abandoned on the Cross, by what right do you seek reassuring truths? I myself have thought about these inspiring truths for a long time. How do you explain this mystery – if you clasp on to such inspiring truths, why are you so sad? The Word gives us some protection, similar to the safety rope used by mountaineers, but it is not of a sheltered type. If I stopped believing in eternal life I would feel as though I were dead to it.

Because I have spoken so often about the after-life in my self-assured manner, about eternal life – in sermons, at conferences – all with perfect sincerity, the tears are welling up in me now. Or if someone falls from grace who is very close to me, someone you might refer to as a friend, do I have any more kind thoughts to offer that he can turn over in his mind, kind words with which to console him? Serious matters and suffering shouldn't necessarily prevent either humour or irony; if you allow them to, you enter into complicity with death itself. It is believed that faith is strong enough to allow the imagination to have some leeway. Or maybe the suffering wasn't intense enough up to this point. When you really love someone and when you bury her in the ground, there are no more images to evoke, no words to say.

The smile that mother assumed in death hadn't fooled me, but I had contrived to interpret it in my own way; in the same way that you can find any meaning you want in a stone or in the clouds in the sky. At one time I would have found such ideas derisory. All the corpses were having a great laugh at me, buried though they were under the earth. What is the hereafter, eternal life? I couldn't say anymore; I had nothing further to add to the discussion. For a long time, in truth, as long as I hadn't really been struck with real force by pain and loss, I had drugged myself with images, with the sweet sound of well-turned phrases, with quotations. I needed to believe, but need isn't sufficient. And yet that appeared to add up to something approaching a totality. Also it kept the dreaded feeling of absurdity at bay. I was now coming up against a smooth wall that you couldn't climb. A faint light, shining in the distance, an almost impersonal prayer that was being said, these were my sole comforts. My faith was nothing more than an opinion, a theme with which to exalt myself. Now that I was helpless, I was trying to cling on to it like the swift currents of a waterfall try to cling on to the rock as they crash down.

Logical reasoning has long since been displaced in my mind. It's strange, but it seemed now that it was mother's silence, her indifference even to all human and religious props, the humility of her eyes in which I believed I saw a boundless astonishment at what was happening to her, and the same look of reproach as I saw in the look of the condemned animal, that were signalling to me now. I will be an object of scandal for you. *Father, why have you abandoned me?* It's no use trying to be with me, leave behind all your projects, your soft words, even your hand that holds mine . . . *Noli me tangere.* You cannot wait up with me. Sleep now. By coming up against the wall of darkness and abandon it seemed to me that she, the simple one, was teaching me what I only knew in an abstract way through words and literature – that faith was played out on a much deeper level than that of our ideas, habits or feelings, and that the true 'Yes' or 'No' we offered to God weren't perhaps truly acceptance or refusal because they were uttered by talkative and healthy people.

I am sounding a solemn note from on high, I know. Even if this type of insight is infinitely important in one way, in another it is a matter of no importance whether or not we are this or that type of person, whether we feel such and such a sentiment, utter such and such a word, or have noble or lowly ideas. Ideas, sentiments, habits and words are only of any use on this earth. All this psychological mumbo jumbo that could as easily hide as reveal our real motivation remains a mystery to other people as well as to ourselves. I was now more fearful of a peaceful death, the serene death of the believer or the unbeliever leaving this world, with their will made, pronouncing words of solace to those they were leaving behind, accepting death or aspiring to the afterlife, planning in advance the funeral service or calculating the number of Masses that should be said for the repose of their soul. These people, it seemed to me, were bypassing mystery by remaining prisoners of appearances right to the end. On the other hand, the death that mercilessly flogged the flesh and overwhelmed reason gave some weight to the Christian dogma that the ultimate grace is *gratis data*, that is to say that death is something totally other than a line you draw under figures that you wish to add up, but rather an invisible battleground where we are beaten before we begin, unless the hand of mercy comes to grab us, because nobody can ensure his own salvation. God alone saves us, the believer and non-believer alike, the pious soul and the strong-willed person, the man of pleasure and the one who is abstemious, because God loves us without logic or reason.

I really should advance with this certitude. I thought I was lucid, clever at detecting lies. I was like a child looking into the chasm of a mystery. I used to tease you about your religion, mother, make speeches to you about it. When you left this life, you taught me more than all the books and all the discourses.

For centuries, the land on this side of the ridge has looked the same. In Tabarja, in winter, at about three o'clock in the afternoon, the birds settle themselves down on the lawn that goes down to the sea, they dig for worms and make chirpy noises for a quarter of an hour before flying off and landing near tamarind and orange trees. In Tiruchi, at around five in the evening, a mass of multi-coloured birds look for food among the mango and filao trees. The bell for silence in a monastery cannot achieve a more immediate or absolute response. Here, at seven in the evening, the travellers return home, the tall pine tree begins to rustle all of a sudden as the wind picks up. The birds, a quarter of an hour later, disappear into the thickets, make a din for three minutes and then enter the reigning silence. And the cattle in the large meadow come and go following the sun. Everything is orchestrated, mother, as if by hand. Like the tide, like the blood running through our veins.

It's just as it used to be in the past, when evening turns to night. The men return from work with their jackets over their shoulders, slightly bowed by the work they have done, struggling to see in the twilight. But then the sonic blast of the passing planes makes the window-frames shake, dogs whine as if they sense an earthquake. And it's almost as if this is to remind us of the expression, *Peace is another form of war.*

Even beside the poorest farms there is a piece of paradise – a tiny patch of lawn, red mushrooms with white spots, yellow ducks, a type of pit made out of old tyres painted in all the colours of the rainbow, and then at the top of a rockery full of sweet peas you'll find a statue of the Virgin of Massabielle. But a few kilometres further on, beyond the ridge, can be heard the roar of the huge combine-harvesters. The paths have been filled in and the trees knocked down, just like at Fontaines noires. The combine-harvesters work at night in the brightness of their huge headlights: the light goes over the ridge, briefly illuminating the skyline. The machine throws out the bails of hay, or the bags of grain that are loaded as they come out onto trailers. The man driving isn't a peasant any more but some sort of exalted mechanic, an astronaut in the world of agriculture. The poetry that dominated our lives in the country has gone, mother. We're just like two shadows from another time, a time that goes back almost to the era of Ruth and Booz, when we went to the gleaning at harvest time, bending down and straightening up among the *quintelles*, the sheaves of wheat lined up alongside each other at various intervals. We would then form *yanes*, a gleaning of about a hundred ears of grain, for whoever was the fastest. When you saw me filch an ear of grain from a sheaf, instead of giving me a lecture you'd take one yourself. We were fellow conspirators. And on our way home you'd lean on me saying, 'You're my little walking stick, to keep me going in my old age!' The poetry that we knew is no longer. We don't care. There will always be children to dream up worlds: poetry is not external; it is within us.

On days when it is very warm and sunny I walk along the river and my footsteps make a dry crackly sound on the ripening wheat. All around me is the song of oats in a low key, like the timbre of crystal as it begins to fade. Getting through the barbed wire, tearing your trousers in the process, bending down to get past electric fences, lifting gates, opening them, closing them again so that they are firmly in position, these are gestures from the past that come back instinctively and stir memories of childhood. While going along the river, accompanied by the death of my mother, I rediscover for a moment the child I once was. The boy who was capable of waiting an hour or two for the earth to move under the burrowing of a mole and to see the latter emerge from his dejection looking neat and silky. Or else the boy who had infinite patience when it came to following the tracks of otters, martens, muskrats and skunks and whose dream it was to see an ermine. When it came to witnessing a fish in the mouth of an otter, a cock being dragged off by a fox, I relentlessly came down on the side of nature. I could recognise the croaking of the toad, with its single clear note, and the way his heart would beat in his neck. And you can give all the scientific proof you want to disprove the theory that the snake hynoptises its prey, I know that it's true. I saw it happen twenty-five years ago on a path that wasn't used too much by the inhabitants of Fontaines noires. The snake had rolled itself up into a spiral and then suddenly raised its head above its coils, while the little robin, its feathers standing on end, went towards the serpent's mouth with little mechanical steps. He had forgotten that he had the whole sky available to him. I knew the names of all the birds, their habits and their songs. I don't know anything anymore. I have begun following pale and insignificant ideas. I used to know everything, but not how to express it, I didn't even begin to think how I would set about conveying my knowledge. This was the eternal order of things to which I was firmly attached. Now that I would like to express what I know, now that I might have the means to achieve it, I know nothing anymore about that knowledge of which I was once so sure.

A few isolated fishermen make their own private kingdoms in the shade of some willow trees. They are the wise ones who know how to relax in the midst of people who never stop running around like headless chickens. They refuse to budge from where they are, or else the idea never occurs to them or they just aren't able to. They're not going to play the death lottery on the roads when all the holiday-makers set out for their various destinations. The river near where I'm spending some time is called *La Sèche*, or maybe it's called *La Seiche* – I'm not sure. The muskrats have dug little tunnels under the meadow, which means you have to watch where you're walking, like when there's snow on the mountains. You never know when your footing will go from under you. The rivers of this area have names that would make you believe they're cursed: *La Sèche* (Dried-up), *La Vilaine* (The Ugly One) and *La Rance* (The Foul-smelling one). The latter only attains some beauty at its mouth. *La Sèche* is nearly completely still at this time of year, a little foul-smelling also like *La Vilaine*. But it still supplies water to enormous poplars, which is sucked into the sky where the trees produce their own wind to cool themselves. The trees on this side of the ridge are still standing. There are a few indistinct, unused paths between the slopes where the flowers that are common at the processions for Corpus Christi still grow. There is little in France more similar to an Indian village than the one we lived in thirty years ago. We formed a world without unrealistic desires, welded together by tradition, poverty, friendship. Here already nearly all the roofs have television aerials that will relay a thousand desires to the occupants and seek to capture and fill their minds with nonsense. Willingly or by force, country people now watch the dramas lived out by rich people, their comedies. You couldn't tell them anything they don't already know about these things. Sceptics, like these modern philosophers you come across all the time now, they will watch, flabbergasted, programs that put forward little modern Rastignacs who are cold-hearted, the perfect products of the modern metropolis. They will end up coming to the conclusion that salvation is to be found in the absence of salvation, that you must, at all costs, enhance your social standing. Finally, mother, they will come to the stage where they are ashamed of God. The holy priests had better start organising as many ceremonies as possible for them – processions, high Masses. They'd need to polish up on their sermons while they're at it.

What a help Bach has been to me! He was so much more helpful than ideas, a marvellous incitement to prayer. His *Ich habe genug*, for example: *I have enough. Oh world, I can no longer stay here.* The oboe explores the torn and tender notes, but the double vibrations of the string instruments balance each other in an almost carefree manner – feelings are not in any way at the origin of peace. Or else there's his *Kreuzstabekantate. My journey in this world is like a voyage on a ship. Come, death, my liberating angel!* The cello sets the sound waves in motion, describes anguish and passion, while the oboe floats effortlessly in the liquid air, laughing, laughing at everything.

How could I have failed to come across Bach for such a long time? It took mother's death to fully appreciate the force of this music. I was particularly suspicious of the Cantatas, which were always dealing with the theme of death. They seemed to me to be the expression of a certain period, to reflect the victories of death, before sending the angels of Fra Angelico floating over the people kneeling in dread and begging for mercy. I had no desire to find again in the Cantatas of Bach the death that I had read in my mother's eyes, and that the sermons of my prolonged adolescence had instilled in me, as well as my daily reading of the *Imitation of Christ.* Above all, I couldn't endure the thought of being offered the images of a peace achieved through death which evolved beyond our control. It seemed to me that man was not made either to look death in the face nor to escape from it

131

through celestial aspirations towards a life that was at a remove from experience. Rather, he needed to find peace once more in his simple existence and to participate in an absolute manner in the mortal love he felt for others. I thought in this way until the day I came to see my error. In my new vision of things, words were of absolutely no use in this world. The man I had now become, beyond the forms that were imposed on him, expressed the experiences that he lived through and assumed death by creating a literary corpus of work.

The music spoke to me – it might have been a flute, an oboe, the clarinet of a cantata, or a human voice, the voice itself was a musical instrument, and the instrument vibrated to the warmth of a voice – the melody was saying nothing, but something was being expressed nonetheless in the depths of my soul, very far away, inaudibly. In this manner, the flute, the oboe or the human voice, separately or together, said something that went beyond emotions and feelings, in complete harmony with the most secret part of each person, which is also the most universal part. It said: 'You are *that*, don't be frightened, the game is up, you are no longer merely in this worldly time, my poor frightened creature. *Jerusalem is no farther from you than your own body.*'

As I was listening to the cantata for the nineteenth Sunday after the feast of the Trinity, for example, I had wondered, long before the event that would change my outlook on life, why the tears would well up when I was not feeling any conscious emotion. And at the same time why a mad joy would rise up from the depths of my soul as I had what could be referred to as an insight of what was to come – the room, the bed, mother's hands joined and the rosary beads tied around them. Or else the vision took the form of the deserted house, the abandoned trees or the things in life that were wrapped up in old friendships. Thus it is that a young man can sense, with the help of a pure morning, in a poem, a melody, a page of Racine or Pascal, a verse of Baudelaire, everything that is to come, the discovery of love, suffering, long periods in the desert, the remedy for his ailments. And when he has this moment of revelation, which is at the same time more and less impressive than the premonition of future events, at the same time more and less arid and desperate, he is amazed at the feeling that he has lived through all that already, in a different way, better, and that if the remedy is successfully completed and the grace is given to him to rediscover his second innocence, it surprises him that it took so many different emotions, passions, excitement, shouts, in order for him to come back to the state of lost unity with God. From this summit he can observe with detachment the ebb and flow of life.

But it wasn't like this in my mother's case. She didn't pray or bless anyone. I had merely formed an image in the manner of Epinal – it was far from being perfectly accurate. It was as if everything had been played out a long time ago and death no longer concerned her. In every gesture of her life this had happened, in every look, every word she spoke. And there I was standing like a stranger, waiting for everything to be over, because in a sense we had said our goodbyes a very long time ago through the window in her house. I had already endured her death even if I hadn't recognised it in the monstrous form it had assumed. I also felt that there was all the time needed in the future for her to become real and to reach me second by second, since it was impossible to live in the present moment.

The music warned me – it could have been Bach or Mozart, maybe even Rachmaninov – that everything was over already, the pleasure and the pain, the meetings and the departures. There was a kingdom deep within each one of us, infinitely far away (although, at this point what was far away or near lost all meaning), a kingdom, a land, where you could live in pain and in joy, in the desert all alone and in the warmth of friendship. Majestic peace reigned in this kingdom. And maybe this fragile kingdom, which seemed to be attached to the soaring of a fugue, the cry of an oboe, had nothing to do with any of this. Or else it could be like a painted surface that hurt you in a pleasant manner, the page or sentence of an unknown author that caused you to close the book and read no more because there was nothing else it could teach you after this.

Or it could be a morning, after days or months in the desert when you were dead inside, in such a lowly state of mind that the only light that reached you was that of an lifeless star, when your fears and hopes seemed like the fears and hopes of another, a morning when you wake up with a rhythm in your head, a sentence burning to be written down, and the world wells up all of a sudden, you have broken through the barrier and know that you need to write, write. Oh God, give me enough time to write down all I want to express!

Then again maybe this kingdom I've talked about had nothing whatever to do with anything I was feeling. This kingdom that seemed to be so attached to a rhythm, to forms, to a phrase, to an obsessive image that not even the dawn could obliterate. Similarly maybe it had nothing to do with the kingdom that is promised by our faith to anyone who remains loyal, nor with this ultimate craving of the heart and of the mind that saves us from contingency, because it is outside of the senses and the imagination. It has to be first of all *nada*, a void, before it becomes plenitude. And yet this zone of peace in the eye of the storm was a premonition, a reference point and obviously a promise that was as real as suffering, more virulent than despair.

Or it could be a country where I was rediscovering a landscape with the same force as when you painfully remember a face. The time comes when the face that has almost been erased comes back into your consciousness to cut through you like a sharp blade – days that had long since faded into the past, so much passion, desperation, so many hopes, plans, risks taken that all helped you to live through the dull moments. While passing, you sneaked by: 'Fortify yourself my soul'. . . There hasn't actually been a shift in time; in the same movement the oboe lords over the cello. Melancholy follows the tearing at the heart by memory like the look on a person's face as they turn around before departing. And the melancholy itself is only the disguised messenger of another grace that opens the door to austere joy; if the past is nothing, it says, if so many reasons for going on living have disappeared, the present isn't important either, no more than your plans, your hopes. Don't therefore try to escape from life, allow yourself to be carried along in its resonant torrent. You live after all in the kingdom of serenity: it's because of your dissimulation that you are nervous. Participate in life, continue to hope, to fear, to love, but like a stranger. Keep yourself joyfully busy until the end of the show, you can feel at home in your own house.

Je vis, je ne sais pour quel temps
Je mourrai, je ne sais quand

Je pars, je ne sais où
Je m'émerveille d'être si joyeux. *

Bach's oboe races through the liquid air like a mad bird. At the gate leading into the cemetery, at the entrance to the Valley of Jehoshaphat, a solitary seagull cries out above the sea and here the Gregorian chant, sung in a child's voice, can be heard:

In paradisum deducant te angeli

One of mother's expressions comes back to me:
'Where will you go on Sundays when I'm . . .'
This was the only time she ever alluded to death.
'Do you know what, I might wait for you in the Valley of Jehoshaphat.'
'No,' she said, 'that would be hard to endure.'
'Well then,' I said, 'don't worry, because you'll be with me every Sunday and I'll make every day Sunday.'
The hereafter is a dense darkness that is heavily populated. Without a doubt, it's better not to imagine it at all. There's too great a risk that in so doing I might forget about the days I have left to live in this life. The deserts of vast eternity are too extensive for me. Every day will therefore be Sunday, Angela, my beloved mother.

* I live, I know not for how long, / I will die, I don't know when, / I am leaving, I don't know where, / How can I be so happy?